Chocolate

Chocolate

PATRICIA LOUSADA

Food styling by Janice Murfitt
Photography by Ian O'Leary

DK Publishing, Inc.

A DK PUBLISHING BOOK
www.dk.com

Art Editor Jane Bull
Editor Janice Anderson
Assistant Editor Lorraine Turner
US Editors Laaren Brown, Joan Whitman,
Irene Pavitt
DTP Designer Bridget Roseberry
Managing Editors Fay Franklin
Mary Ling
Deputy Art Director Carole Ash
Production Manager Maryann Rogers

First American paperback edition, 1999
2 4 6 8 10 9 7 5 3 1

Published in the United States by
DK Publishing, Inc.,
95 Madison Avenue, New York, New York 10016

DK Publishing books are available
at special discounts for bulk
purchases for sales promotions or
premiums. Special editions, including
personalized covers, excerpts of existing
guides, and corporate imprints can be
created in large quantities for specific
needs. For more information, contact
Special Markets Dept./DK Publishing,
Inc./95 Madison Ave.
/New York, NY 10016/Fax: 900-600-9098

Library of Congress
Cataloging-in-Publication Data
Lousada, Patricia
Chocolate/Patricia Lousada.
p. cm.
Includes index.
ISBN 0–7894–2084–8 (hc) Published as
Ultimate Chocolate
ISBN 0-7894-4838-6 (pb)
1. Cookery (Chocolate) I. Title.
TX767.C5L6823 1997   97-13144
641.6'374 - - dc21   CIP

Reproduced by Colourscan, Singapore
Printed and bound in Singapore by Star
Standard Industries (Pte.) Ltd.

Contents

Introduction

Chocolate is one of the world's most delectable foods and the one that most satisfies our desire for something sweet. Its special rich flavor can create the most delicious cakes, cookies, ice creams, and other desserts and even savory recipes. When we think of a treat to please, we think of chocolate.

Where Chocolate Comes From

Chocolate is made from the bean of a tree, *Theobroma cacao*, native to the tropical areas of Central and South America. Thousands of years before it arrived in Europe, the Maya and Aztecs were brewing it as a drink, offering it to their gods during tribal rituals and using it for currency. The Aztec emperors kept vast storehouses of cocoa beans, which they used as treasuries.

When Columbus returned from the New World in 1502, bringing cocoa beans for the king of Spain, no one showed much interest in them. Twenty years later, after conquering Mexico, Cortez also brought cocoa to Spain. He had first tasted it at the Mexican court of Montezuma in a cold, bitter drink called *xocolatl* (bitter water). This was made with chilies and other native flavorings and was topped with a foamy froth created by the cocoa butter.

South American Indian with chocolate pot and cup

In Mexico, the Spanish conquistadores adopted the Aztecs' practice of using the cocoa beans for wage and market transactions, but it took longer for them to get accustomed to the bitter drink.

Over time, thanks to intermarriages between the two cultures, the unpalatably bitter drink evolved. It was sweetened with sugar, flavored with Old World spices such as cinnamon and anise, and served hot. Another refinement was the *molinillo*, a wooden swizzlestick used to whip the cocoa into a froth. The Aztecs had favored a method of pouring the drink from one vessel to another to create the foam.

Europe Discovers Chocolate

In this new form, cocoa was successfully introduced into Spain. It was a drink for the elite, who took to it for its medicinal effects as well as for its taste. Over time, the new drink's popularity spread. Missionaries who had been to South America brought it back to monasteries and convents in Italy and southwest France. It trickled into court life through the intermarriage of royal families. In 1660 the Infanta Maria Theresa of Spain married the king of France, Louis XIV. She and her retinue were fond of chocolate, and the personal maid who prepared it was nicknamed "la Molina" by the French court. Within ten years, chocolate was well established at Versailles and throughout French aristocratic and intellectual circles.

A noble French family takes chocolate

We can get an idea of how splendidly it was served from Madame D'Aulnoy, a French visitor to the court of Spain. In 1679 she wrote:

"They presented next Chocolate, each cup of porcelain on a saucer of agate garnished with gold, with the sugar in a bowl of the same. There was iced chocolate, another hot and another with Milk and Eggs, one took it with a Biscuit, or rather with dry small buns...."

For two and a half centuries, controversy raged within Catholic countries as to whether the taking of chocolate broke the ecclesiastical fast. Was it food to nourish the body or a beverage to quench thirst? The Jesuits, who traded in chocolate, held that it did not break the fast; the Dominicans took the opposite view.

When chocolate appeared in England in the middle of the seventeenth century, chocolate houses became important meeting places for the fashionable and well-to-do. Samuel Pepys wrote in his diary of enjoying "jocalatte," and writers including Addison and Steele mention the chocolate houses in their works. The drink was an expensive luxury, so heavily taxed by the government that cocoa beans were often smuggled into the country. When Gladstone lowered the chocolate tax in 1853, prices fell, and even the less affluent could now enjoy chocolate.

English covered chocolate cup, ca. 1805

Drinking Chocolate Becomes Eating Chocolate

Until 1828, cocoa for drinking was manufactured by grinding the beans into a "chocolate liquor" and adding spices and sugar, as well as some kind of farinaceous substance to soak up the cocoa butter, which tended to float to the top. A major breakthrough occurred in that year when Dutch chemist Coenraad J. Van Houten invented a press to extract cocoa butter from the bean, leaving a dry cake that could be ground into an almost fat-free cocoa powder similar to that of today. Van Houten's press was used in England by the leading chocolate manufacturers of the day. Two of these companies were owned by prominent Quaker families, Cadbury and Fry. It was they who, twenty years later and as a direct result of this innovation, produced the first eating chocolate.

In North America, too, the early cocoa manufacturers are still among today's leaders. In 1765, Dr. James Baker joined forces with a newly arrived Irish cocoa maker and started the now-famous Baker's company. Domenico Ghirardelli, drawn to California by the gold rush, opened a chocolate factory in San Francisco in 1849. It continues to produce chocolate, and the landmark buildings that once housed its company are known as Ghirardelli Square. Hershey, too, is a household name; Milton S. Hershey founded a whole town in Pennsylvania as a result of his chocolate success. Like something out of a child's fantasy, Hershey, Pennsylvania, has streets named Cocoa and Chocolate Avenue, and lampposts shaped after his famous kisses.

How Chocolate Is Made

As the world's appetite for chocolate increased — and it is still increasing today — manufacturing methods improved to meet the growing demand. Turning cocoa beans into edible chocolate is a long and complicated process. It begins, of course, on the plantations, which are always located within twenty degrees of the equator. Even at this latitude, the trees will not be productive if the altitude is too high or the temperature falls below 60°F (16°C). They also require a rain forest

Cocoa pod and beans

atmosphere where midges thrive, as they are the only insects that pollinate the small five-petaled flowers. Cocoa trees start producing their fruit when they are four to five years old. The beans, or seeds, grow in spindle-shaped pods that form on the trunk and thickest branches of the tree. The pods are harvested twice a year and split open at once with a machete, so the beans can be scooped out and left to dry in the sun. An average tree yields only one or two pounds of dried beans a year, since the beans lose 50 percent of their weight during drying. There are two main varieties of beans: the Forastero, a high-yielding bean that provides 80 percent of the world's cacao crop, and the Criollo, a superior-flavored bean that is often blended with the Forastero to improve its flavor. There are also a number of hybrid beans, of which the Trinitario is the best known. Each manufacturer processes its own beans using an individual formula. The overall process, however, is the same throughout the world. The beans are roasted to bring out their flavor and then cracked so their protective shells and husks can be removed, leaving the kernels, called nibs. Once the nibs have been exposed, they must be ground. The friction of the grinding melts the cocoa butter in the nibs and extracts most of it, leaving a thick paste called chocolate liquor. This liquor, cooled and hardened, is unsweetened cooking chocolate. If the liquor is then pressed, more cocoa butter will be released from it, and the remaining hard mass, ground to powder, becomes cocoa.

All chocolate liquor retains some of its original cocoa butter content. To form sweetened chocolate, extra cocoa butter is added to the liquor along with sugar and flavorings, such as vanilla. Milk chocolate, now made with dried milk, was originally created in 1875 using condensed milk. We owe the smooth texture of chocolate as we now know it to a Swiss manufacturer named Rodolphe Lindt, who invented "conching." Until 1880, all eating chocolate had a rough, grainy texture. Lindt increased the amount of cocoa butter in his chocolate recipes. In his conch-shaped machine, the enriched liquor was blended repeatedly over several days — much longer than was customary. The result of this innovation was the smooth, creamy chocolate we know today.

Advertisement for chocolate, 1913

Chocolate and Good Health

The effects of chocolate on health have long been debated. Too much sugar, we know, is not good for us. A fine-quality dark chocolate has only a small amount of sugar and a large amount of nutrients, such as calcium, potassium, riboflavin, niacin, and vitamin A. Recent research has found that chocolate's high level of phenol is helpful against heart disease. As for keeping us awake, compared with the 75–175 milligrams of caffeine in a cup of coffee, cocoa has a meager 25 milligrams to none at all.

Chocolate is an obsession with some people and irresistible to most of us. Its botanical name, *Theobroma cacao*, means "food for the gods," but ordinary mortals seem to become addicted to chocolate just as easily. Monthly magazines have even been devoted to it, printed with chocolate-scented ink. Perhaps word had spread that Madame de Pompadour recommended chocolate as an aphrodisiac, and Casanova rated it above champagne for its seductive qualities.

Successful Cooking with Chocolate

The recipes in this book give clear, step-by-step instructions to help you achieve perfect results. However, there are some essential rules that should be followed carefully.

◆ Measure and prepare all ingredients before you start work on a recipe.

◆ Always use ingredients at room temperature; take eggs, butter, and milk out of the refrigerator in good time (but not cream for whipping, or it will separate).

◆ Follow the same units of measurement throughout; do not mix imperial and metric.

◆ All spoon measurements are level: 1 teaspoon = 5ml; 1 tablespoon = 15ml.

◆ All eggs are large unless otherwise stated.

◆ The correct-size baking pan is important for cakes and pies. Measure across the top of the pan from one inside wall to the other. Disregard any other measurement marked on the pan.

◆ Turn on the oven before starting to make a recipe and make sure that it has reached the correct temperature before use.

◆ To ensure that the oven temperature is correct, check with an oven thermometer placed in the center of the oven before putting in the dish to be baked.

◆ Baking times given in the recipes can only be a guide, because every oven varies. Check the dish 5 minutes before the end of the recommended cooking time, and leave in the oven or remove as necessary.

✳ **Warning: Raw or very lightly cooked eggs can transmit salmonella. Recipes with this warning should not be given to the elderly, young children, and pregnant women.**

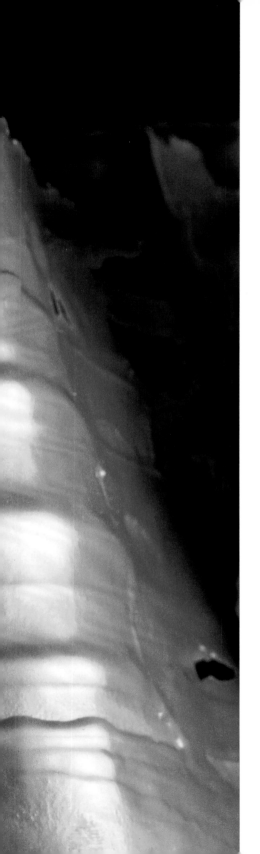

A Gallery of
Chocolate

These pages of gorgeous, taste-bud-tingling chocolate cakes, desserts, confectionery, tarts, cookies, and rich sauces give a preview of *Ultimate Chocolate*'s wonderfully wide-ranging contents. They illustrate recipes drawn from the cooking and baking traditions of many countries and cover all the ways in which chocolate may be used in cooking. Whichever dishes you choose to make, you are certain to give pleasure to everyone who loves chocolate.

Marbled Millefeuille
(See pages 106–7.)

Chocolate Layer Cakes

Above and opposite:
Pecan Chocolate Fudge
Cake (*See page 56.*)

Nothing tempts the chocolate lover's tastebuds as thoroughly as a layer cake extravagantly filled with a chocolate buttercream crunchy with nuts, thickly whipped cream, or a fruit-flavored frosting. There is plenty of choice here, from classics like Black Forest Cake to everyone's favorite, Chocolate Layer Cake.

"On no other occasion has Nature concentrated in so small a space [the cocoa bean] such an abundance of the most valuable nourishment."

Alexander von Humboldt,
19th-century traveler

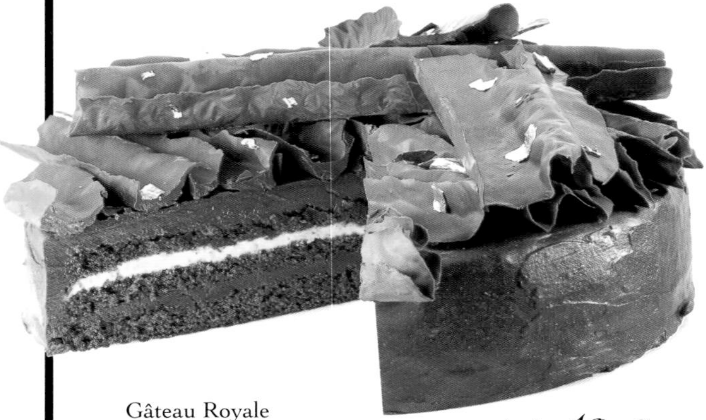

Gâteau Royale
(*See pages 58–9.*)

White Chocolate Cake
(*See page 61.*)

Below:
Black Forest Cake
(*See page 57.*)

Deliciously dark chocolate cake, sandwiched with rich creamy fillings and frostings

Dessert Cakes

Above and opposite:
Chocolate Truffle Cake
(See page 71.)

Stylishly decorated and richly flavored dessert cakes and tortes have been a well-loved theme in Continental patisserie for generations. This irresistible selection brings together some of the greatest chocolate dessert cakes, including the classic Sacher Torte and a deliciously soft-textured Chocolate Truffle Cake.

"When I die," I said to my friend, "I'm not going to be embalmed. I'm going to be dipped." "Milk chocolate or bittersweet?" was her immediate concern.

Adrianne Marcus, *The Chocolate Bible* (1982)

Sacher Torte
(See page 72.)

Le Diabolo
(See page 73.)

See the glories of chocolate unfold in myriad decorative shapes and many melt-in-the-mouth textures. Delight in the luscious curls and lightly trailing whirls, the delicately veined leaves and finely drawn scrolls.

Celestial Kumquat Torte
(See page 68.)

Chocolate Hazelnut Cake
(See page 70.)

Cookies

Above and opposite:
Chocolate Hazelnut Tuiles
(See page 89.)

Chocolate cookies make the perfect snack, ideal with a glass of milk or cup of coffee, or just nibbled and relished on their own. Others are excellent accompaniments for desserts and ice creams. Most cookie recipes are easy to make – although the decorating can be as elaborate as you like – and they store well, too.

"I observe my chocolate diet, to which I believe I owe my health.... It is admirable and delicious."

Marie de Villars,
wife of a French
ambassador, 1680

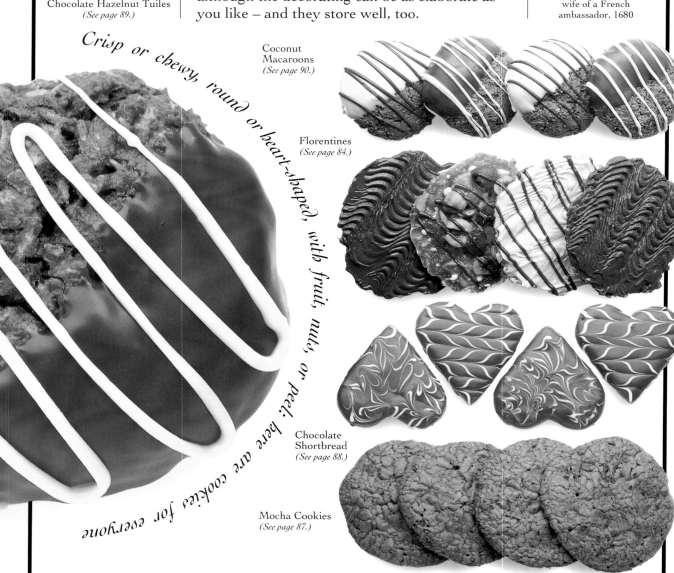

Crisp or chewy, round or heart-shaped, with fruit, nuts, or peel, here are cookies for everyone

Coconut
Macaroons
(See page 90.)

Florentines
(See page 84.)

Chocolate
Shortbread
(See page 88.)

Mocha Cookies
(See page 87.)

Pies & Tarts

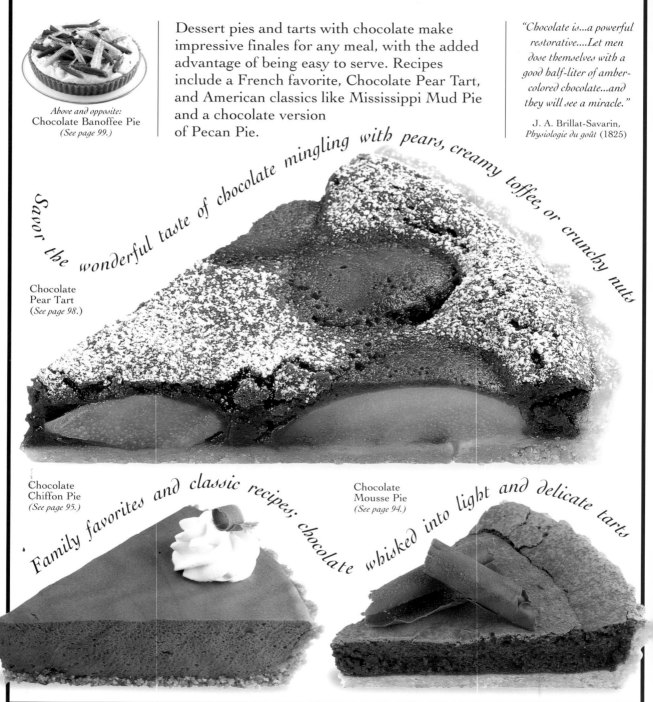

Above and opposite:
Chocolate Banoffee Pie
(See page 99.)

Dessert pies and tarts with chocolate make impressive finales for any meal, with the added advantage of being easy to serve. Recipes include a French favorite, Chocolate Pear Tart, and American classics like Mississippi Mud Pie and a chocolate version of Pecan Pie.

"Chocolate is...a powerful restorative....Let men dose themselves with a good half-liter of amber-colored chocolate...and they will see a miracle."

J. A. Brillat-Savarin,
Physiologie du goût (1825)

Savor the wonderful taste of chocolate mingling with pears, creamy toffee, or crunchy nuts

Chocolate
Pear Tart
(See page 98.)

Chocolate
Chiffon Pie
(See page 95.)

Family favorites and classic recipes: chocolate whisked into light and delicate tarts

Chocolate
Mousse Pie
(See page 94.)

Cold Desserts

Cold chocolate desserts and ices, however elaborate, can be prepared well in advance, making them ideal for dinner parties and special occasions. A beautifully presented layered chocolate terrine, scoops of chocolate mousse with a luscious sauce, or a stunning iced soufflé will guarantee a successful finale to any meal.

"Chocolate is not only pleasant to taste, but it is a veritable balm of the mouth."

Dr. S. Blancardi, Amsterdam physician, 1705

Above and opposite:
White Chocolate and Lime Mousse *(See page 108.)*

Black and White Hazelnut Mousse
(See page 115.)

Chocolate Meringue Sandwich
(See page 110.)

Marbled Millefeuille
(See pages 106–7.)

Cool chocolate in mousses and soufflés; light-as-air chocolate layers in elegant terrines; ice-cold chocolate in frozen desserts and ice creams

White Chocolate Ice Cream *(See page 120.)*

Confectionery

Above A basket of Truffles and Candies

Fudge, responsible for awakening many a childhood interest in cooking, is just one of a variety of sweets that can be made at home. Mints, chocolate-covered nuts, and Italian panforte are within any cook's range. Chocolate truffles are perhaps the easiest and most delicious of all—and they look sumptuous, too.

"The sweets I remember best were...filled with dark chocolate filling. If I found one now I am sure it would have the same taste of hope."

Graham Greene, writer

White chocolate-dipped Truffle *(See page 124.)*

Armagnac Prune Truffle *(See page 122.)*

Chocolate Truffle coated in grated chocolate *(See page 124.)*

White Chocolate Truffle *(See page 125.)*

Chocolate Truffle *(See page 124.)*

Irresistibly stylish sweets and truffles filled with fruit, nuts and liqueur creams

Chocolate Truffle coated in cocoa powder *(See page 124.)*

White Chocolate Truffle with chopped nut coating *(See page 125.)*

ChocolateTruffle *(See page 124.)*

Truffle with white chocolate decoration *(See page 124.)*

Chocolate Sauces

Above and opposite:
Bitter Chocolate Sauce
(See page 135.)

Sauces have an important role to play with sweet dishes. Whether it is a hot fudge sauce to be poured over ice cream, a warm chocolate sauce to serve with steamed pudding, or a sharp raspberry coulis to contrast and mellow the richness of chocolate, sauces stimulate our visual appreciation as well as our palates.

"To a coffee-house, to drink jocolatte, very good."

Samuel Pepys,
Diary (1664)

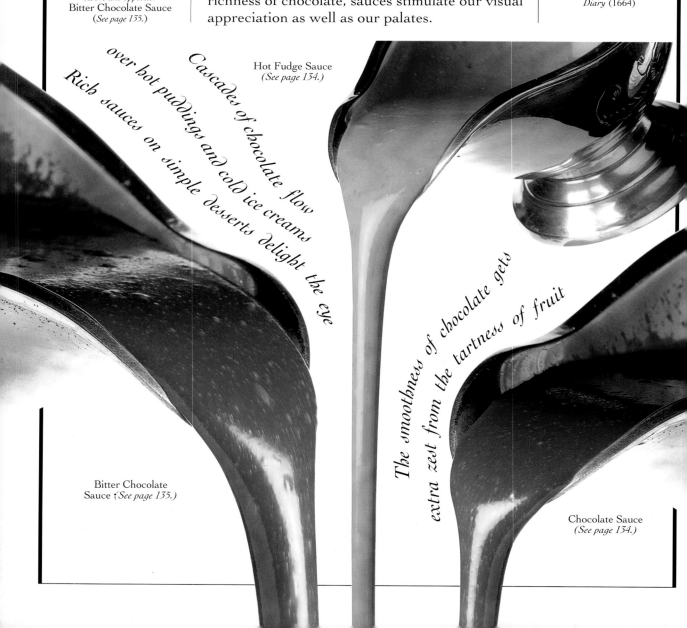

Hot Fudge Sauce
(See page 134.)

Cascades of chocolate flow over hot puddings and cold ice creams Rich sauces on simple desserts delight the eye

The smoothness of chocolate gets extra zest from the tartness of fruit

Bitter Chocolate
Sauce *(See page 135.)*

Chocolate Sauce
(See page 134.)

The Essentials of
Cooking
with
Chocolate

Chocolate is an exciting ingredient to work with, especially when its unique properties are understood and the techniques of handling it have been mastered. This section deals with both. The different types of chocolate are described and illustrated, with detailed information on how each is best used in cooking. The basic techniques of chopping, melting, and tempering chocolate are shown in clear step-by-step sequences. Also included are hints on buying and storing chocolate and on the essential kitchen tools and equipment needed for successful cooking with chocolate.

Melting chocolate
(See page 33.)

Making Chocolate

Chocolate, like coffee, originates in a bean, but one that grows on a tree, not a bush. The exotic cocoa tree produces a blizzard of pink and white flowers, green unripe fruit, and bright golden cocoa pods, all at the same time.

Encased in the pod is the dark little cocoa bean. Put through an intricate production process, the bean is transformed into cocoa mass, which ultimately becomes that magically pleasurable ingredient, chocolate.

THE COCOA TREE

The region between the twentieth parallels, with the exception of parts of Africa, is the home of the cocoa tree. The tree begins to bear fruit once it is four years old and has an active lifespan of at least sixty years. Its fruit grows directly out of the older wood of the trunk and main branches, reaching the size of a small football and ripening to a rich golden color. Inside the ripe pods, purplish-brown cocoa beans are surrounded by pale pink pulp. After the pods are cut from the tree, beans and pulp are left to ferment together. The beans turn a dull red and develop their characteristic flavor. After fermentation, the beans are dried in the sun, acquiring their final "chocolate" color. They are now ready for shipping to the manufacturing countries. Various bean types have been bred, and experts take pride in their ability to distinguish chocolate made from Criollo or Trinitario beans from that made from Forastero.

PROCESSING THE BEANS

When the dried beans reach the processing plant, they are cleaned and checked for quality, and then roasted. Roasting, an important stage in the manufacturing process, develops the flavor of the beans and loosens the kernels from the hard outer shell. Each chocolate manufacturer has its own roasting secrets, which contribute significantly to the chocolate's flavor. After roasting the beans have a distinctive chocolaty smell. The next step is to crack the beans open, discarding their shells and husks to obtain the kernels, called nibs. It is the processing of these small brown nibs that gives us chocolate. The roasted nibs, which contain on average 54 percent cocoa butter, are ground into a dark, thick paste called cocoa mass or solids. When more pressure is applied to the cocoa mass, the resulting products are cocoa butter and a solid cocoa cake. From the cocoa cake, when it is crushed into cocoa crumbs and then finely ground, comes cocoa powder.

Cocoa pod (left)

Dried cocoa bean (above)

Cocoa butter

Cocoa solids, or mass

Cocoa crumbs

CONCHING

Chocolate is generally cocoa solids and sugar, with added cocoa butter (in the case of semisweet chocolate), or milk (in the case of milk chocolate), plus vanilla and other flavorings. Conching, in which the chocolate mixture is heated in huge vats and rotated with large paddles to blend it, is the final manufacturing process. Small additions of cocoa butter and lecithin, an emulsifier, are made to create the smooth, voluptuous qualities essential to the final product.

SWEETENING CHOCOLATE

Baking or bitter chocolate is simply cocoa solids and cocoa butter. To produce the great range of chocolates, from bittersweet to semisweet to sweet, more cocoa butter plus varying amounts of sugar, vanilla, and lecithin are added. The flavor and sweetness of a chocolate will be unique to its maker, with one brand's bittersweet tasting like another brand's semisweet. Changing your usual brand of chocolate can make a difference in the flavor of a favorite recipe. To make milk chocolate, milk solids replace some of the cocoa solids. White chocolate is not, in fact, a real chocolate since it is made without cocoa solids; brands containing all cocoa butter, rather than vegetable oil, are best.

BUYING AND STORING CHOCOLATE

◆ Read the label. "Artificial chocolate" and "chocolate–flavored" are not the real thing, as both flavor and texture will confirm.

◆ Note the percentages of cocoa solids and sugar on the label: they indicate the quality and taste of the chocolate.

◆ Store chocolate tightly wrapped in plastic wrap, in a cool, dry, airy place, preferably at a constant temperature.

◆ Properly stored bitter or semisweet chocolate will keep for over a year.

◆ Milk and white chocolate should not be kept for more than six months. Although the latter may taste fine, it does not melt well after long storage.

◆ Stored at warm temperatures, chocolate will develop a "bloom" of surface streaks and blotches; at damp, cold temperatures, a gray-white film may form. These changes will not greatly affect the flavor and texture of the chocolate, and it can still be used for cooking and baking.

Types of Chocolate

SEMISWEET CHOCOLATE

A great range of excellent eating (dessert) and cooking chocolate is available in supermarkets as well as specialty shops. Differences between brands depend on the beans used, the proportion of cocoa solids and cocoa butter, and the sugar content and flavoring. The darkest chocolate contains the highest proportion of cocoa solids and cocoa butter, with chocolates called continental containing up to 75 percent cocoa solids. A good semisweet chocolate has a minimum of 45–50 percent cocoa solids. Less expensive brands substitute vegetable oils and shortening for the cocoa butter.

Semisweet chocolate is the type most commonly used as a baking ingredient.

COCOA POWDER

There are two types: the more mellow Dutch-process or alkalized, and nonalkalized. The two are interchangeable in cooking. Sweetened cocoa powder is not a substitute.

CHOCOLATE CHIPS

Designed to keep their shape without melting during baking, they cannot replace cooking chocolate.

COUVERTURE

Also called dipping or coating chocolate, this fine-quality chef's chocolate is tempered before use as a coating chocolate (see page 35). Because of its high cocoa butter content, it melts smoothly and sets to a thin coating with a high gloss when it has been tempered. It is available in semisweet, white, and milk chocolate varieties, in blocks and as chocolate drops.

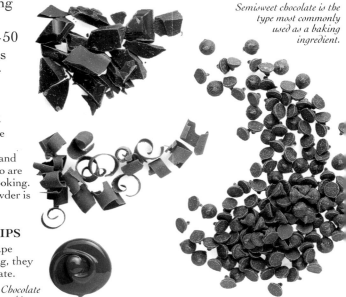

Chocolate chips

Couverture

Plain chocolate, variously called bittersweet, semisweet, dark and continental dark, or plain, is the main chocolate for cooking. All but bittersweet contain enough sugar to make them sweet enough to eat.

Different brands contain varying amounts of cocoa solids and sugar. Check the package label and use a brand that contains a minimum of 45–50% cocoa solids. Bittersweet or dark chocolate contains as much as 75% cocoa solids.

MILK CHOCOLATE

Milk chocolate is often used as a decorative chocolate, making a perfect color and taste contrast with semisweet chocolate.

WHITE CHOCOLATE

White chocolate has an extra sweet flavor that makes it popular for making confectionery.

In milk chocolate, milk solids (dried milk or condensed milk) replace some of the cocoa solids, giving it a sweet taste and smooth texture. The best brands are those that contain the highest percentage of cocoa solids and real vanilla.

Milk chocolate is not suitable for cooking. It is more sensitive to heat than semisweet chocolate, making it difficult to work with. It is very useful for decoration, however, making a good contrast to semisweet in both color and flavor.

White chocolate is technically not a real chocolate, since it does not contain cocoa solids. Better brands are made with a high proportion of cocoa butter as well as milk solids and sugar. Avoid those made with vegetable oil or fat.

As with milk chocolate, white chocolate does not tolerate heat and is usually melted but not baked. The added milk solids can cause it to turn grainy when heated too quickly. Its sweet but delicious flavor makes it popular with dessert chefs.

Basic Techniques

Chocolate is simple to work with, but needs careful handling. Knowing how to chop, grate, melt, and temper chocolate correctly is the key to success because these techniques are basic to cooking and to making chocolate decorations. Master them and you will make deliciously simple desserts and adventurous chocolate creations with ease.

Chocolate is sensitive to atmosphere. Cool, dry air provides the best conditions for working with it. If your kitchen is hot and steamy, chocolate will be difficult to handle. Avoid this problem by planning your chocolate baking or cooking session for a time when other cooking in the kitchen has been completed.

CHOPPING AND GRATING

Chocolate to be chopped or grated must be firm; chill it briefly before beginning. If you are grating or chopping by hand, handle the chocolate as little as possible, using a piece of paper to prevent it from melting from the heat of your hands. Chop or grate onto a clean, dry surface, as moisture will affect the consistency of the chocolate if it is to be melted. To grate, use a large piece that is easy to handle, hold it firmly, and work against the large grid of the grater.

Chop with a knife that has a large, sharp blade. Use the broad end, not the tip, and rock the edge of the blade over the chocolate until pieces break easily. Cut chocolate into even-size pieces.

Fit a food processor with a metal blade. Put chocolate pieces into the machine, and then use the pulse button to chop. Do not overwork, as the heat of the machine could melt the chocolate.

MELTING CHOCOLATE

Follow the method for melting chocolate described on page 33. Once the chocolate starts to melt, stir it occasionally until it is smooth, and then remove it from the heat. Chocolates have different consistencies when melted: for example, bittersweet chocolate becomes runny, while semisweet and dark chocolates hold their shape until stirred. Thus, a chocolate may keep its shape when it is already soft and in danger of getting too hot. Keep heat low (no more than 110°F/44°C) to stop scorching and ruining the flavor.

Melting in a Microwave Oven
The inside of the microwave must be completely dry. Break the chocolate into even-size pieces before putting it into a bowl for melting. Timing will depend on the output of the oven and the type and amount of chocolate being melted, but never melt chocolate on High. The chart on the right gives timings for a 650-watt oven; for ovens with a higher wattage, timings may be about 30 seconds less. Stirring the chocolate every 30 seconds during melting will enable you to keep a check on progress.

APPROXIMATE MELTING TIMES IN A 650-WATT MICROWAVE OVEN

Semisweet Chocolate

Quantity	On Medium
2oz (60g)	2 minutes
4oz (125g)	2½ minutes
6oz (180g)	3 minutes

Milk and White Chocolate

Quantity	On Low
2oz (60g)	2½ minutes
4oz (125g)	3 minutes
6oz (180g)	4 minutes

SUCCESSFUL MELTING

Chocolate should not be melted over direct heat. A double boiler or a water bath, made by putting a metal or glass bowl over a pan of water, is the best method. The bottom of the bowl should not touch the water in the pan.

This chocolate is just starting to melt

1 Break or chop the chocolate into even-sized pieces and put in a metal or glass bowl. Smaller pieces will melt more quickly.

2 Put the bowl over a pan of hot, but not simmering (bubbling), water. Once the chocolate starts to melt, stir it occasionally to push unmelted pieces into the melted chocolate.

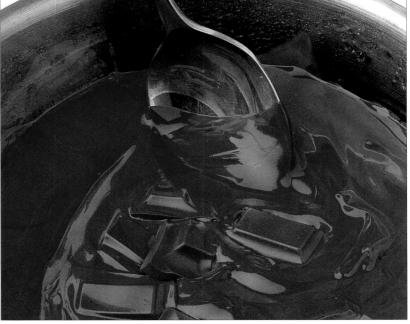

3 When completely melted, chocolate should have a smooth, glossy texture. Chocolate that has been allowed to overheat will separate, or "seize," turning into a rough mass. Rescue seized chocolate by stirring in 1 teaspoon warm vegetable oil, repeating if necessary.

PREPARING MELTED CHOCOLATE FOR CURLS AND CUTOUTS

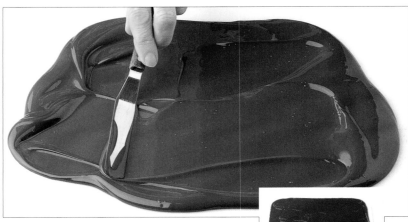

1 For decorations such as curls, caraque, and cutouts, pour melted chocolate onto a clean, smooth work surface such as an acrylic board.

2 Using a narrow spatula, spread the chocolate across the surface with even strokes. The chocolate should be of a uniform thickness so it sets evenly.

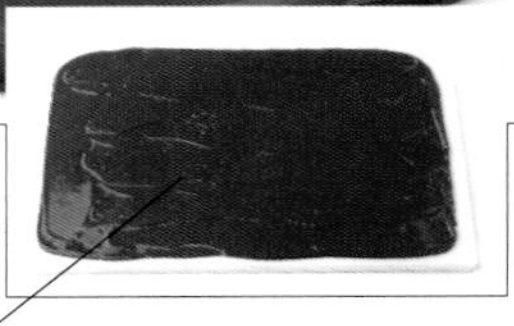

Spread chocolate to about 1/16in (1.5mm) thick

MELTING CHOCOLATE WITH OTHER INGREDIENTS

Butter or oil can be melted with chocolate or added during melting without putting it at risk. Chocolate can be melted with a liquid as long as there is enough of it – at least 1 tablespoon of liquid per 2oz (60g) of chocolate.

Ingredients for melting with chocolate must be at a similar temperature. Adding a hotter liquid can cause the chocolate to seize. Adding a cold ingredient straight from the refrigerator can make the chocolate lumpy.

COMBINING MELTED CHOCOLATE WITH OTHER INGREDIENTS

Many recipes include a step where chocolate is melted, or combined in its melted form, with other ingredients. Here are some simple tips to follow:

◆ Let melted chocolate cool to room temperature before adding it to cake mixtures and cookie doughs. If the chocolate is too hot, it can melt the fat in the mixture and cause a change in the texture of the final baked product.

◆ Melted chocolate added to a light mixture, like creamed sugar and butter, should be whisked in quickly in a warm place to keep the chocolate fluid.

◆ Use a wooden spoon to mix melted chocolate into a thick mixture like egg yolks and sugar. Steady the bowl while beating in the chocolate.

◆ In a microwave, chocolate takes less time to melt with butter or liquid than when melted on its own.

◆ White chocolate has a tendency to seize easily. It should be treated with extra care when being melted or combined with any ingredient.

1 Remove the butter from the refrigerator ahead of time so that it is at room temperature before being used. Melt the chocolate, and then remove it from the heat.

2 Gently stir the butter into the melted chocolate with a rubber spatula to ensure a smooth texture.

TEMPERING COUVERTURE

The tempering process prevents couverture from looking dull and streaky once it has been melted and then solidifies. Melted couverture is mixed with other ingredients in recipes. When couverture is used on its own for coating and decorations, the tempering gives it a crisp, glossy finish that remains shiny for weeks without refrigeration. The chocolate also shrinks slightly, allowing it to be released easily from a mold.

1 Melt the chopped chocolate (see page 33). Stir the melting chocolate gently until the temperature reaches 113°F (45°C) on a chocolate thermometer and the consistency is very smooth.

2 Pour three-quarters of the chocolate onto a cool, smooth work surface, such as an acrylic board or a marble slab. Spread evenly with a palette knife. The surface must be clean and dry.

Spread evenly with a small spatula

3 Work the chocolate using a plastic scraper or spatula, spreading it back and forth across the board and then back over itself.

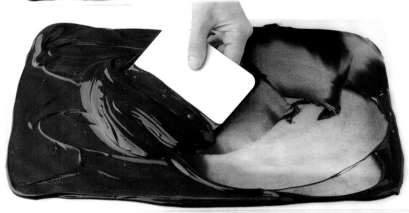

4 After a few minutes of being worked, the chocolate will have cooled and thickened. Check the temperature; the chocolate is ready when the chocolate thermometer reads 82°F (28°C).

5 Return the chocolate to the bowl. Set the bowl over a saucepan of hot water and stir the chocolates gently together with a rubber spatula.

6 Stir the chocolate constantly over the hot water until its temperature has returned to 90°F (32°C); the chocolate should be smooth and glossy.

7 The tempered chocolate should be used at once. Keep it over warm water to retain the correct temperature. It can be tempered again, if necessary.

Essential Tools

Here is a selection of useful equipment for cooking with chocolate. Several items, found in most kitchens, are included here because they are essential to specifically chocolate-related techniques.

When buying tools, always choose the best quality available: they last longer, are more reliable, and achieve the best results. Once you are familiar with the techniques in the book, your own essentials will be added to this list.

Acrylic board

Vegetable peeler makes curls easily

Wooden spoon

Metal spoon

Large chef's knife

A vegetable peeler and a grater are everyday kitchen tools that are also useful for cooking with chocolate. The large grid of the grater makes small chocolate curls and grates chocolate. The vegetable peeler also makes chocolate curls.

Mixing and stirring heated ingredients is best done with a long-handled wooden spoon. Use metal spoons for folding in flour and whisked egg whites. Flexible rubber spatulas scrape every bit from the sides of a bowl.

Stainless steel box grater

A knife for chopping chocolate should have a long broad blade with a sharp edge. A clean acrylic board has many uses. Use it to spread out chocolate when making decorations and tempering. A marble surface sometimes allows chocolate to cool and harden too quickly.

Long-handled rubber-bladed spatula

Candy thermometer

A saucepan and a heatproof bowl that fits firmly into it make a perfect water bath for melting chocolate. Choose a glass bowl that allows you to monitor the hot water in the pan: it must not bubble.

Chocolate thermometer

Thermometers should be well tested before using. The small red-topped thermometer is a chocolate thermometer. The large candy thermometer is an essential tool when boiling sugar syrups for buttercreams and some cakes.

Bowls made of strong heatproof glass with smooth, rounded bottoms are best for melting chocolate in a microwave or a water bath.

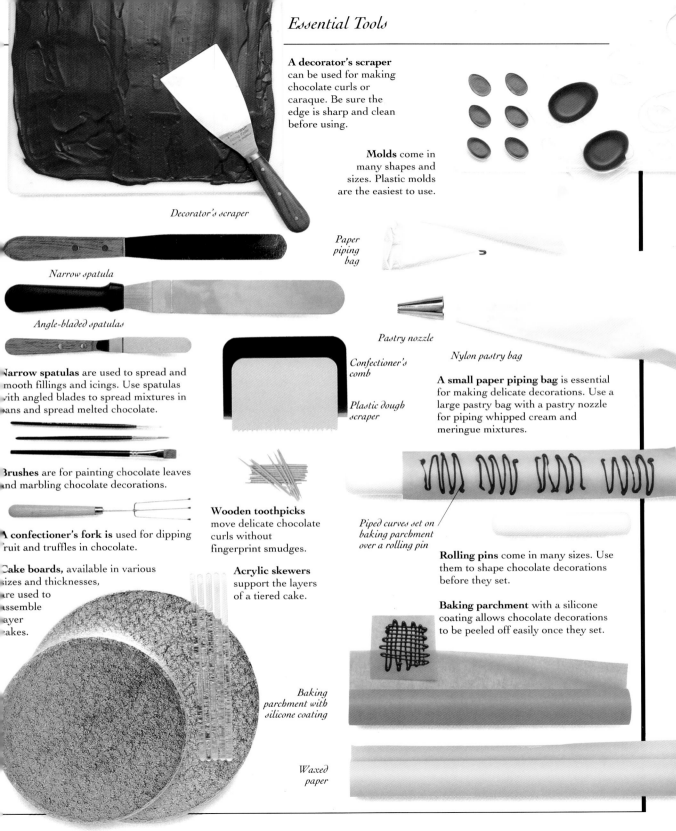

Essential Tools

A decorator's scraper can be used for making chocolate curls or caraque. Be sure the edge is sharp and clean before using.

Decorator's scraper

Molds come in many shapes and sizes. Plastic molds are the easiest to use.

Narrow spatula

Angle-bladed spatulas

Paper piping bag

Narrow spatulas are used to spread and smooth fillings and icings. Use spatulas with angled blades to spread mixtures in pans and spread melted chocolate.

Confectioner's comb

Pastry nozzle

Plastic dough scraper

Nylon pastry bag

A small paper piping bag is essential for making delicate decorations. Use a large pastry bag with a pastry nozzle for piping whipped cream and meringue mixtures.

Brushes are for painting chocolate leaves and marbling chocolate decorations.

Wooden toothpicks move delicate chocolate curls without fingerprint smudges.

A confectioner's fork is used for dipping fruit and truffles in chocolate.

Piped curves set on baking parchment over a rolling pin

Rolling pins come in many sizes. Use them to shape chocolate decorations before they set.

Acrylic skewers support the layers of a tiered cake.

Cake boards, available in various sizes and thicknesses, are used to assemble layer cakes.

Baking parchment with a silicone coating allows chocolate decorations to be peeled off easily once they set.

Baking parchment with silicone coating

Waxed paper

Working with Chocolate

Dos & Don'ts of Melting Chocolate

◆ Do cut chocolate into even-sized pieces to melt.

◆ Don't melt chocolate over direct heat.

◆ Do use a water bath with a glass bowl so you can check that the water does not bubble too strongly.

◆ Don't allow the hot water to touch the bowl.

◆ Do melt chocolate slowly to achieve the smoothest results.

◆ Don't cover the bowl of chocolate while it is melting; condensation forming under the cover could drop into the chocolate and damage it.

◆ Do wipe the inside of the microwave completely dry before using it to melt chocolate.

◆ Do watch milk and white chocolates carefully; they will burn and seize more easily than semisweet.

◆ Do melt chocolate with a good quantity of liquid, – at least 1 tablespoon per 2oz (60g) of chocolate.

◆ Don't forget to have all ingredients at room temperature before starting a recipe.

What do I do when chocolate turns lumpy?

◆ Chocolate that has become lumpy or grainy can be rescued by stirring in 1 or 2 teaspoons of vegetable oil until smooth.

Is there any way to save chocolate once it has been scorched or burned?

◆ When chocolate is heated over direct heat, or a water bath gets too hot too quickly, chocolate will burn. Once the flavor of the chocolate has been affected, it cannot be saved.

What if I've carefully melted chocolate with a safe amount of liquid and I know it hasn't burned, but it seizes anyway?

◆ Chocolate that has turned grainy and hard can sometimes be rescued by adding extra liquid to loosen it. The water or other liquid should be the same temperature as the seized chocolate and should be added 1 tablespoon at a time. Add each tablespoon all at once and whisk vigorously. Repeat if necessary.

Preparing Chocolate for Decorations

When do I need to temper my chocolate? What happens if I don't?

◆ It is not necessary to temper chocolate, whether semisweet or couverture, when it is used in everyday cooking. Tempered couverture is essential to achieve a professional, glossy finish on confectionery and chocolate decorations. This finish also allows confectionery to be kept at room temperature without losing its glossy luster.

◆ Couverture that is untempered will "bloom," becoming dull and streaky, when it dries.

Can I use untempered couverture for decorating or covering confectionery?

◆ No, because it may become streaky. It is better to use a good-quality semisweet chocolate that does not need tempering.

When making chocolate curls, what should I do if the chocolate splinters instead of curling?

◆ This means that the chocolate is too hard. Wave a hand-held hair dryer, on the lowest temperature, over the chocolate for a few seconds. Try again.

When making chocolate curls, what should I do if the chocolate melts and sticks to the scraper?

◆ This means that the chocolate is too soft. Put the board of chocolate into the refrigerator for 30–60 seconds to harden a little. Try again.

When should I refrigerate a finished chocolate recipe and when should I avoid the refrigerator?

◆ Put decorations and dipped confections made with untempered chocolate in the refrigerator immediately after they are made. This "freezes" the fat crystals, and preserves the glossy finish.

◆ Tortes and cakes that have been glazed and stored at room temperature after making will be ruined if they are later put in the refrigerator. Chilling makes them dense and hard and dulls the finish of the glaze.

PREPARING CAKE PANS

The correct size and type of pan is crucial to successful cake baking. Preparing a cake pan helps to stop the cake from sticking, making it easier to remove. Odd-shaped pans should be greased twice with butter, and then dusted with flour. Line other pans with baking parchment, which has a nonstick finish, or waxed paper, which needs to be brushed with more butter.

HELPFUL TIPS

- *All bakeware should be clean and dry before you start.*
- *Greasing before lining keeps the paper in place.*

1 Brush the inside of the pan evenly with melted butter. Cut one strip of paper to fit around the sides, overlapping slightly, making sure it is 2in (5cm) wider than the depth of the pan.

2 Fold in one long edge of the paper by 1in (2.5cm) and crease well. Unfold and then make angled cuts at 1in (2.5cm) intervals along this edge, up to the folded line.

3 Drop the paper strip cut side down into the pan so that the creased edge rests in the seam at the base of the pan. Press the paper well onto the buttered sides and bottom of the cake pan.

4 Place the bottom of the pan on another piece of paper. Draw a faint pencil line around the base. Cut out the circle just inside the pencil line so the paper disk fits snugly into the bottom.

5 Smooth the paper circle on the bottom of the pan, making sure that the cut edge lies flat underneath it. If using waxed paper, brush once more with melted butter.

TOASTING AND SKINNING HAZELNUTS

Hazelnuts seem to have a special affinity for chocolate, and the two are combined in several recipes in this book. Toasting hazelnuts allows their papery skins to be removed easily.

1 Preheat the oven to 350°F (180°C). Spread the nuts on a baking sheet. Bake for 8 minutes.

2 Shake the hot nuts onto a cloth. Fold the cloth over them and rub gently to remove the skins. Cool before using.

Decorating
with
Chocolate

It is the decorative touches – curls, fans, ribbons, flowers and leaves, curves, waves, and cutouts – that personalize chocolate cakes, desserts, and cookies, making them uniquely special. This section explains how to make many kinds of decoration with a professional finish, from easily made simple effects with melted chocolate to more elaborate decorations based on piping chocolate, including feathering, marbling, and other patterns. Making and using fillings and coverings, which are essential bases for many decorations, complete the section in impressive style.

Marbled Chocolate Eggs
(See page 129.)

Making Decorations

Chocolate decorations enhance the appearance of desserts and cakes and offer opportunities for creating original displays of chocolate perfection. The decorations here, all of them used in recipes in this book, cover a wide range, from easy to intricate.

Elaborate decorations, such as piped shapes and marbled curls, require practice to master. Others, like cutout shapes and leaves, are easier for the beginner to tackle. Take a free afternoon to practice making decorations. Always start with chocolate that is firm and at room temperature, since cold chocolate cracks easily and too soft chocolate can become sticky. Trial runs will not waste expensive chocolate, since failed efforts can go back into the melting bowl, and any items successfully completed can be kept for several days or weeks, until the opportunity arises to use them. Most decorations can be stored in an airtight container in the refrigerator. They may also be frozen, separated between sheets of waxed paper. Wrap larger pieces, such as baskets, waves, and large curls, in plastic wrap before putting them in containers. Milk and white chocolate decorations will keep for two weeks in the refrigerator; couverture and semisweet chocolate ones will keep for four weeks.

GRATED

Grated chocolate, an easily made decoration

1 Use a large piece of chocolate that is easy to handle. Chill the chocolate in the refrigerator briefly to firm it before grating. If your hands are very warm, hold the chocolate in a piece of paper to prevent melting.

2 Work the chocolate against the large grid of the grater, as in the picture above. Grate the chocolate onto a plate or waxed paper.

Note: As an alternative, a food processor fitted with a grater disk can also be used. Break chocolate into chunky pieces. Feed the pieces of chocolate through the feeder tube while the machine is running.

QUICK CURLS

For wide curls use the flat underside of the peeler

Store between sheets of waxed paper in the refrigerator

Curls are quickly made with a vegetable peeler

1 Use a large, thick bar of chocolate at room temperature. Scrape the chocolate firmly along its length with a sharp, swivel-type vegetable peeler. For narrow curls, use one of the edges; for fat curls, use the flat underside of the peeler.

2 If curls splinter or crack, the chocolate is too cold. Rub the chocolate with your thumb to soften it a little. If the chocolate becomes too soft, put it in the refrigerator briefly.

Note: Pressure applied on the block of chocolate will also affect the size of the curls. Applying firm pressure will result in larger, sturdier curls.

CARAQUE

Using a large-bladed knife to make caraque

1 Spread chocolate on an acrylic board (see page 34). Let it set firmly. Have a large-bladed knife ready.

2 Brace the board against your body. Starting about 2in (5cm) from the left corner of the board farthest from you, pull the knife blade toward you at a 45-degree angle, scraping along the chocolate to form a caraque, as shown above.

3 Use the knife blade to lift each piece of caraque off the board as you make it.

Note: For striped caraque, spread stripes of different colored chocolates, touching, on the board.

CURLS

Chocolate fans /

Making curls with a decorator's scraper

1 Begin with a work surface spread with a thin layer of chocolate (see page 34). Allow the chocolate to set firmly at room temperature before starting. Have ready a decorator's scraper that is thoroughly clean.

2 Start 1in (2.5cm) from the nearest edge of chocolate. Push the decorator's scraper away from you at a 25-degree angle across the surface of the chocolate until a large curl forms, as shown above. Use the scraper to lift the curl off the board as it is made.

3 To form fans, push the scraper forward, and then pull it at a sharp angle, about 10 degrees, to one side.

LEAVES

Real leaves are used to make this decoration

1 Use pliable leaves with well-defined veins, such as rose leaves. Artichoke leaves are excellent for making large roses. Be sure the leaves are chemical-free, cleaned, and dry.

2 Hold the leaf by its stem and use a small paintbrush or pastry brush to coat a smooth layer of melted chocolate on the underside of the leaf, as shown above. Be careful not to drip chocolate over the edge of the leaf, or it will be difficult to peel off.

3 Place, coated side up, on a baking sheet lined with baking parchment, and refrigerate until set. Peel leaf away from the chocolate (see the insert).

RIBBONS

Piped lines of white chocolate decorate these ribbons, used on the Wedding Cake (see pages 66–7)

Set the ends of longer ribbons into an egg carton to turn them upward

Ribbons become curved when set over a rolling pin

1 Cut nonstick baking parchment into strips the width and length of the ribbons you plan to make.

2 Allow 4oz (125g) melted chocolate for about a dozen ribbons ¾in (1.5cm) wide and 6in (15cm) long.

3 Holding each end of a paper strip, dip just one side of the strip into the melted chocolate to coat it.

4 Lay the coated strip over a rolling pin to form a curve, as shown above. If desired, also put the ends of long ribbons into egg carton compartments to turn them upward. Allow to set, then peel off the paper.

WAVES

Melted chocolate sets into waves over chopsticks

1 Cut plastic bubble wrap or baking parchment into pieces the width of the waves you are planning to make.

2 Melt 2oz (60g) chocolate for a wave approx. 9 x 12in (23 x 30cm). Lay three chopsticks slightly apart on a work surface. Secure each one in place with tape, as shown above.

3 Spread the bubble wrap or parchment with a thick layer of melted chocolate. Arrange over the sticks, as shown in the picture above; secure one end to the board with tape.

4 Allow to harden. Carefully peel off the wrap just before using.

BASKETS

Use a small, angled narrow spatula to spread chocolate evenly

Chocolate baskets set into pretty folds

1 Cut plastic bubble wrap or baking parchment into four pieces, each 5in (12cm) square.

2 Melt 4oz (125g) chocolate to make four baskets. Spread the squares of bubble wrap or baking parchment with a thin layer of chocolate, leaving a narrow border.

3 Holding the squares by their clean corners, set each one gently into a small, shallow bowl or wide-mouthed glass or goblet, as shown above.

4 Put the bowls in the refrigerator until ready to use. Carefully peel the wrap away from the chocolate.

CUTOUTS

Gently peel back the baking parchment from the chocolate

A sharp knife easily cuts the chocolate into shapes

1 Melt semisweet chocolate. Cut two pieces of baking parchment large enough to cover your work board.

2 Put one piece of parchment on the board and spread it with melted chocolate in an even layer about 1/16 in (1.5mm) thick.

3 Allow to cool at room temperature. Once the chocolate is firm, flip the work board and the chocolate-coated parchment paper over onto the second piece of parchment.

4 Peel the paper away from the chocolate. Cut into desired shapes with a sharp knife, as shown above.

BOXES

For the box, cut two 4in (10cm) squares for the base and lid; cut four sides 4 x 1in (10 x 2.5cm) (cut 2 sides a little wider for overlap)

Melted chocolate holds the box's pieces together

1 This marbled chocolate box (shown with truffles on page 123) requires 5oz (150g) semisweet chocolate and 2oz (60g) white chocolate.

2 Melt the semisweet chocolate and spread it in a thin layer on a 7 x 9in (18 x 23cm) piece of baking parchment. To create the marbling with the white chocolate, see page 47.

3 Trim the chocolate and cut it into rectangles (see above for sizes). Melt chocolate trimmings. Use this chocolate to brush along the outside edges of the bottom rectangle, as shown above. Attach the sides to the bottom by cementing with the melted chocolate.

COMBING

Use prongs of a fork to make wavy lines

This melted chocolate decoration includes piping (see page 46)

A fork quickly combs a pattern into chocolate

1 Use a confectioner's comb or a fork to make an attractive decoration on cookies like Florentines (see page 84).

2 Melt semisweet, milk, or white chocolate or, for a stunning effect, tempered couverture.

3 Hold the cookie between thumb and forefinger and dip its base gently into the melted chocolate.

4 Put it on a wire rack, chocolate side up. When the chocolate is slightly set, gently drag the comb or fork across the chocolate, using a wavy motion, as shown above.

MAKING A PIPING BAG

Melted chocolate and thin icings are easily piped with a homemade paper piping bag. Cut a very small opening in the tip of the bag so that you can control the flow of the chocolate.

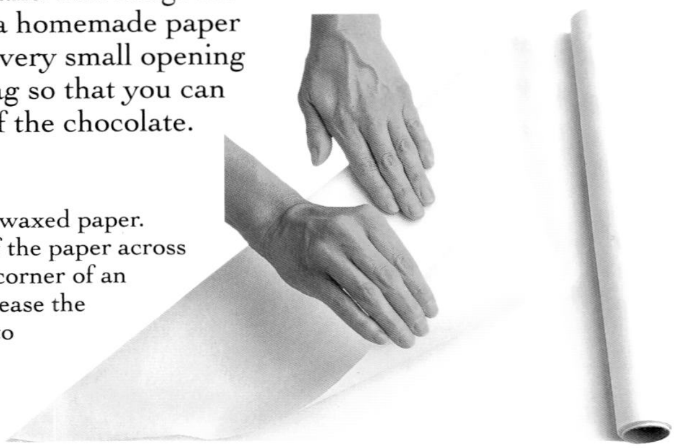

1 Unroll a length of waxed paper. Fold one corner of the paper across to meet the opposite corner of an imaginary square. Crease the fold and cut along it to remove a triangle of paper.

2 Fold the triangle in half. Place on a flat surface, with its long side facing you. Bring the right-hand point up and across to meet the middle point.

3 Now, fold the paper twice to the left to meet the left point. Squeeze the cone to open. Fold down the top edge of the cone above the seam to secure.

4 Open the cone and gently spoon the icing into the finished bag. For best results, fill the bag just halfway.

5 Fold over the top to seal, turning in the corners. Snip off the tip when ready to use. Hold the cone upright to prevent the icing from running out.

PIPING CHOCOLATE

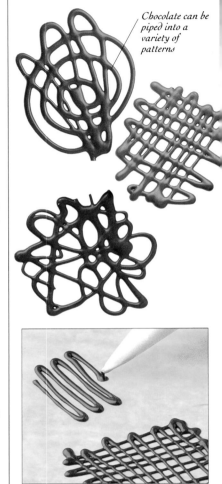

Chocolate can be piped into a variety of patterns

Piping patterns onto baking parchment

1 Sketch a series of simple patterns onto baking parchment. Turn the paper over and put on a baking sheet.

2 Spoon cooled, melted chocolate into a paper piping bag so it is no more than half full. Seal the bag and snip off a small piece of the tip.

3 Pipe the chocolate evenly onto the paper, using the lines of your patterns as a guide, as shown above.

4 Allow the chocolate to set, and then remove the outlines from the paper by gently lifting them off with a narrow spatula.

CHOCOLATE CURVES

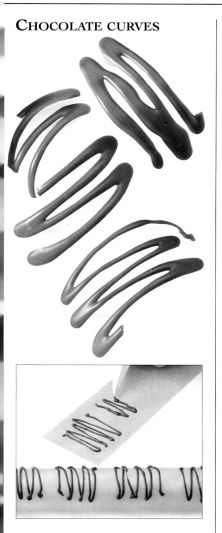

Piped curves are set over a rolling pin

1 Melt some semisweet chocolate and cool it so it just coats the back of a spoon. Half fill a paper piping bag, and then seal it and snip the tip.

2 Pipe lines backward and forward across a strip of silicone-coated baking parchment, as shown above.

3 Carefully lift the strip of baking parchment and place over a rolling pin, as shown. Secure the strip in place with tape.

4 Allow the chocolate to set. Remove the curves by lifting the strip off the rolling pin and then gently peeling paper away from the chocolate curves.

FEATHERING

Feathering lines of chocolate with a toothpick

1 Melt some white chocolate and cool it until it just coats the back of a spoon. Half fill a paper piping bag with the chocolate, seal, and snip tip.

2 Glaze the top of a cake or a batch of cookies with melted semisweet chocolate.

3 While the chocolate glaze is still wet, pipe evenly spaced parallel lines of melted white chocolate over the plain chocolate.

4 Draw the tip of a toothpick through the white chocolate, first in one direction and then in the other, as shown above.

MARBLING

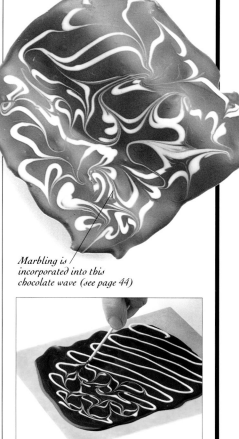

Marbling is incorporated into this chocolate wave (see page 44)

Marbling must be done on wet chocolate

1 Melt some white chocolate and cool it until it just coats the back of a spoon. Half fill a paper piping bag with the chocolate, seal, and snip tip.

2 Melt some semisweet chocolate. Cut a piece of baking parchment and spread with the chocolate, leaving a narrow border clean.

3 While the semisweet chocolate is still wet, pipe a fine line of white chocolate in a looped scribble across the full width of the chocolate.

4 Draw the tip of a toothpick through the white chocolate lines to make swirls, as shown above.

MOLDED FLOWERS

This rose has chocolate marzipan leaves (see page 76)

Fitting rose petals around the central cone

1 Use either commercial chocolate modeling paste or chocolate marzipan (see page 76). Roll a small piece into a cone shape about 1in (2.5cm) long for the center of the rose.

2 Pinch off pea-size pieces of paste or marzipan and flatten between thumb and forefinger into petals, gently turning back the tips. Make some petals larger than others.

3 Fit one petal around the cone, as shown above, and then add others so that each new petal partially covers the one before it, as in the completed roses at top. Finish the rose with large petals around the outside.

FILLING A PASTRY BAG

A nylon pastry bag fitted with a nozzle is best for piping whipped cream and thick buttercreams. A medium star nozzle is a good all-purpose size to choose.

To pipe rosettes, hold the bag upright and pipe in a circular motion to form a peaked swirl

1 Drop the nozzle into the bag, pushing it firmly into the end. Hold the bag halfway up and fold back excess fabric over your hand.

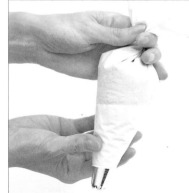

2 Half fill the bag, pushing the icing or cream down to remove air pockets. Unfold the fabric and twist it tightly just above the filling.

Rope design   *Shell design*

Squeeze the bag gently from the top when piping cream or icing

3 Squeeze the top of the bag with a firm and even pressure. Retwist the bag as it empties to keep the filling together at all times.

Fillings and Toppings

A smooth covering of icing can turn a simple cake into an elegant conclusion to the perfect meal or into an appealing centerpiece for a buffet. Add luster to a cake by using a simple glaze: the glossy coating can become the blank canvas for additional decorations. Use the techniques explained here to create flawless finishes and scrumptious fillings.

HOW TO MAKE A GLAZE

Adding a glaze, such as the Chocolate Glaze on page 136, to a cake gives it an elegant and glossy mirrorlike finish. The glaze can be poured directly onto the cake, as with the Celestial Kumquat Torte on page 68. For an even smoother, finer finish, ice the cake with a preliminary coat of cooled, partially set glaze, and glaze it again with the rewarmed mixture, as with the Chocolate Hazelnut Cake on page 70.

1 Break chocolate into pieces. Melt chocolate with butter and corn syrup in the top of a double boiler or over a water bath.

2 Set aside and allow it to cool to a spreadable consistency (it should coat the back of a spoon). Use the glaze according to the recipe being followed.

GLAZING A CAKE TWICE

Giving a cake a preliminary coat of glaze holds crumbs in place and creates an even base for the final glossy coating.

1 Cool the glaze to a spreadable consistency (it should coat the back of a spoon). Use a narrow spatula to spread about a quarter of the glaze over the top and sides of the cake.

2 Allow the glaze to set firmly; reheat the remaining glaze and pour it over the top of the cake for the final finish.

Reheat the glaze to a pourable consistency to cover

Put cake on a wire rack set over a plate to catch the drips from the glaze. Excess glaze can be rewarmed and used again

CHOCOLATE GANACHE

This classic chocolate cream, for which the standard recipe is given on page 136, is used as a deliciously rich filling and as a covering for layer cakes, roulades, choux pastry, and meringues. The recipe on page 136 can also be used as a sauce. The cream and chocolate should be whisked together only until they are blended. The method for making ganache described here is not suitable for using when making ganache as a sauce.

1 Melt the chocolate (see page 33) and set aside to cool. Whip the heavy cream until it forms soft peaks. Fold a large spoonful of cream into the cooled chocolate.

2 Fold the chocolate mixture into the remaining whipped cream. The ganache is best used soon after it is made. Makes enough to fill and cover one double layer cake.

CHOCOLATE FROSTING

There are many recipes for chocolate frosting. The methods may differ, but the basic recipe is much the same. This book's basic recipe uses equal amounts of chocolate and cream, plus butter for a silky result, as with the Pecan Chocolate Fudge Cake on page 56, or milk for a lighter texture, as with the Chocolate Almond and Raspberry Roulade on page 63. The basic proportions used here are 12½oz (350g) chocolate, 1½ cups (350ml) heavy cream, and 3 tablespoons butter.

1 Break the chocolate into even-size pieces and put it into a bowl. Bring the cream to a boil and pour over the chocolate. Stir gently to blend.

2 Cut the butter into small cubes and stir it into the mixture. Beat the mixture with a wooden spoon or wire whisk until thick enough to spread.

CUTTING CAKE IN LAYERS

Place the cake on a firm, level surface. Rest one hand lightly on top of the cake to hold it steady. Slice the cake horizontally through the center with a sharp, long-bladed, serrated knife. When there are several layers, start with the top layer. Carefully separate the layers by sliding a thin cake board between them. Lift off and set aside.

FILLING AND ICING A CAKE

1 Begin with the bottom layer. Spread a portion of the filling evenly to within ¼in (5mm) of the edge of the layer. Put a second cake layer on top, pressing it down gently.

2 Use a narrow spatula to spread the icing in an even layer over the top of the cake, using a paddling action so that the icing runs smoothly down the sides of the cake.

3 Use a generous amount of icing and make light, even strokes with the spatula in order to cover the sides cleanly without spreading crumbs into the finished icing.

FINISHING THE SIDES OF A CAKE

While the glaze is still sticky, decorate the sides of an iced cake with grated chocolate, chopped nuts, or praline. Balance the cake on the palm of one hand. Hold it over a plate of coating. Lift coating onto sides of the cake with a large narrow spatula, pressing gently so the coating stays in place.

MAKING ALMOND PRALINE

1 Measure out ⅓ cup (100g) granulated sugar and 1 cup (100g) shelled unblanched almonds.

2 Oil a marble surface or baking sheet. Put the nuts and sugar in a small heavy-based saucepan. Set the pan over low heat until the sugar starts to melt.

3 Continue cooking, stirring occasionally with a wooden spoon, until the sugar caramelizes and is a deep golden color. The nuts

should make a popping sound as they toast.

4 Pour the praline quickly onto the prepared surface. Spread out and leave until cold and hard.

5 Break into pieces and grind to the required consistency in a food processor or blender.

6 The praline will keep for several weeks in an air-tight container at room temperature.

A COMBED FINISH

After a cake has been covered with a smooth icing, the sides can be marked into horizontal lines with a confectioner's comb. Hold the comb vertically and drag it quickly but firmly through the set covering. The technique is not suitable for glossy icings.

Recipes

Here are more than one hundred delectable recipes, all demonstrating the unique qualities of chocolate, as a food and as an ingredient in cooking. There are recipes for everything from cakes and cookies to handmade chocolates and spectacular desserts, and recipes specially devised for important occasions like birthdays and weddings, or annual celebrations such as Easter, Christmas, and Valentine's Day. There are many North American and traditional favorites as well as more recently created recipes.

Gâteau Royale
(See pages 58–9.)

Rich Layer Cakes

Layer cakes, richly filled and sumptuously decorated, tempt the eye as well as the taste buds. The layer cakes here range from the light sponge of the airy-textured Gâteau Royale to the intensely dark Pecan Chocolate Fudge Cake. In other cakes, the layers are not so obvious: two roulades turn single layers of cake into wheels within wheels, and a pound cake twists chocolate and vanilla layers into each other for a marbled effect. Ending this section is the ultimate layer cake: a beribboned, three-tiered Wedding Cake.

Chocolate Layer Cake

A very quick and easy cake to make and one of my family's favorites. The cake, which has the texture of a firm brownie, is sliced into thin layers, sandwiched together with whipped cream.

INGREDIENTS

For the cake

½ cup (125g) unsalted butter
½ cup (60g) cocoa powder, sifted
2 eggs
1 cup (250g) superfine sugar
1 tsp vanilla extract
½ cup (60g) all-purpose flour
½ cup (60g) self-rising flour

For the filling and decoration

2 tbsp milk
2 cups (450ml) heavy cream
2 tbsp superfine sugar
½ tsp vanilla extract
semisweet chocolate curls (see page 43)

1 Melt the butter in a saucepan over low heat, then stir in the cocoa until blended. Set aside. Beat the eggs with the sugar and vanilla until light, then stir in the cocoa mixture.

2 Sift the flours together twice. Sift them over the egg mixture, a third at a time, folding each one in with a metal spoon. Turn into the prepared pan and bake in the preheated oven for 40–45 minutes, or until a skewer inserted in the center comes out clean.

3 Run a knife around the inside edge of the pan and leave the cake for 10 minutes before turning out onto a wire rack to cool completely. When the cake is cold, wrap it in foil and chill overnight. Although this is not absolutely necessary, it makes the cake easier to slice.

4 With the cake at room temperature, cut it into four equal layers, using a long serrated knife (see page 50). The cake layers will be very thin, so use two narrow spatulas to move them.

5 For the filling, add the milk to the cream and whip until it forms soft peaks. Fold in the sugar and vanilla.

6 Use the top layer, cut side up, as the base. Cover it with some of the cream. Add a second layer and cover with cream; repeat with a third layer. Finish with the bottom layer, cut side down. Cover the top and sides of the cake with the remaining cream and decorate with chocolate curls.

VARIATION
Chocolate Praline Layer Cake
Use 1 quantity praline (see page 51). Fold 8 tablespoons (120g) praline into two-thirds of the whipped cream. Use the plain whipped cream for one layer and the praline cream for two. Cover the top and sides of the cake with the rest of the praline cream. Use the remaining praline to coat the sides of the cake (see page 51). Decorate the top with chocolate curls.

Oven temperature
350°F/180°C

Baking time
40–45 minutes

Baking pan
8in (20cm) cake pan, greased and bottom-lined

Makes
8–10 slices

Storage
Unfilled cake keeps for 4–5 days, wrapped, in the refrigerator; filled cake keeps for 3 days in the refrigerator

**CHOCOLATE PRALINE
LAYER CAKE**
*Almond praline adds a
sophisticated touch to the
Chocolate Layer Cake.*

Pecan Chocolate Fudge Cake

This is a wonderfully rich, moist cake, delicious served with crème anglaise, vanilla ice cream, or just plain whipped cream. Be sure to serve the cake at room temperature, when the texture of the cake and its chocolate flavor will be at their best and most intense.

Eye-catching chocolate ribbons, dusted with cocoa, top this cake

INGREDIENTS

For the cake

4½oz (140g) semisweet chocolate
2½oz (75g) bittersweet chocolate
6 tbsp (90g) unsalted butter
5 eggs
¾ cup (180g) superfine sugar
1 tsp vanilla extract
¾ cup (90g) all-purpose flour
½ tsp salt
¾ tsp baking powder
3 tbsp sour cream or buttermilk

For the frosting and decoration

1½ cups (150g) pecans
6oz (180g) bittersweet chocolate
6oz (180g) semisweet chocolate
1½ cups (350ml) heavy cream
3 tbsp unsalted butter
semisweet, milk, and white chocolate ribbons (see page 44)
cocoa powder

1 For the cake, melt both chocolates and the butter together (see page 34).

2 Put the eggs, sugar, and vanilla in a large bowl set over hot water. Whisk until the eggs have doubled in volume and thickened. Stir in the chocolate mixture.

3 Sift the flour, salt, and baking powder together three times. Sift the flour over the chocolate mixture, a third at a time, folding in each part carefully. Fold in the sour cream or buttermilk.

4 Pour the mixture into the prepared pan. Bake in the preheated oven for about 55 minutes, or until a skewer inserted in the center comes out clean. Set the cake in the pan on a wire rack for 10 minutes; turn out onto the wire rack to cool.

5 For the frosting, lightly toast the pecans in the oven for about 10 minutes. Coarsely chop them.

6 Break both chocolates into a bowl. Bring the cream to a boil and pour over the chocolate. Stir gently to blend. Stir in the butter. Set aside 1 cup (250ml) of the mixture and stir the chopped pecans into the rest. Beat both mixtures until thick enough to spread.

7 Cut the cake into three layers (see page 50) and put one layer on a thin cake board or flat serving plate. Use the pecan frosting to sandwich the layers together. Cover the top and sides of the cake with the plain frosting (see page 51). Decorate the cake with chocolate ribbons and a dusting of cocoa.

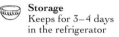

Oven temperature
325°F/160°C

Baking time
55 minutes

Baking pan
9in (23cm) cake pan, greased, lined with greased baking parchment, and floured

Makes
16 slices

Storage
Keeps for 3–4 days in the refrigerator

Freezing
1–2 months, unfilled and undecorated

Black Forest Cake

An impressively tempting chocolate cake layered with an irresistible combination of cherries, cream, and kirsch. Fresh cherries, with their leaves, make an attractive decoration.

INGREDIENTS

For the cake

8 eggs
¼ cup (200g) superfine sugar
1 tsp vanilla extract
7oz (200g) bittersweet chocolate
½ cup (125ml) water
1¼ cups (150g) all-purpose flour, sifted

For the filling and decoration

2lb (1kg) fresh cherries, preferably morello or sour, washed and pitted
⅓ cup (90g) granulated sugar
4 tbsp lemon juice
4 tbsp water
⅔ cup (150ml) kirsch
5 cups (1.25 liters) heavy cream
2 tbsp superfine sugar
semisweet chocolate caraque (see page 43)
whole fresh cherries and leaves

1 Break the eggs into a large heatproof bowl, preferably a copper one, and gradually beat in the sugar, using an electric hand-held beater. Set the bowl over hot water and beat for 6–8 minutes, until the mixture has doubled in volume and is thick enough to leave a ribbon trail when the whisk is lifted. Beat in the vanilla extract.

2 Melt the chocolate and the water together (see page 34). Sift the flour over the egg mixture, a third at a time, folding in each batch carefully with a large metal spoon. Fold in the warm, but not hot, melted chocolate.

3 Divide the mixture evenly between the prepared pans and bake in the preheated oven for 30–35 minutes, or until a skewer inserted in the center comes out clean. Leave the cakes in the pans for a few minutes, then slip a knife around the edges and turn the cakes out onto a wire rack to cool.

4 For the filling, put the cherries in a pan and add the granulated sugar, lemon juice, and water. Simmer over very low heat until the cherries have slightly softened, about 5 minutes (sour cherries will take longer). Strain and reserve the juices. Mix ¼ cup (75ml) of the strained juice with ⅓ cup (90ml) of the kirsch and set aside.

5 Whip the cream until it forms soft peaks, beat in the sugar, and fold in the remaining kirsch.

TO FINISH THE CAKE

1 Cut each cake into two layers (see page 50). Put one layer on a thin cake board or flat cake plate and sprinkle with 3 tablespoons of the kirsch syrup. Cover with a sixth of the whipped cream. Press half the cherries evenly over the cream. Put a second cake layer on top and repeat the syrup, cream, and cherries layer.

2 Put a third cake layer on top, sprinkle with the remaining kirsch syrup, and spread with a layer of cream. Cover with the last cake layer. Spread the top and sides with the remaining cream.

3 Complete the decoration by pressing the chocolate caraque into the cream around the sides of the cake and arranging the fresh cherries and leaves on top.

4 Chill the cake for 2–3 hours before serving in thin slices. To slice, cut with a knife heated in hot water and then dried.

Oven temperature
350°F/180°C

Baking time
30–35 minutes

Baking pans
Two 9in (23cm) cake pans or springform pans, greased, lined, then greased and floured

Makes
12–16 slices

Storage
Keeps for 5 days in the refrigerator, unfilled and undecorated. Completed cake keeps for 3 days in the refrigerator.

Freezing
2 months, unfilled and undecorated

Fresh cherries add a perfect finishing touch

Gâteau Royale

A class of its own! This elegant cake is a true classic. A light Genoese sponge is layered with whipped cream, and there is a rich, mousse-like chocolate frosting to fill and cover the cake. Lavish rolls of chocolate waves, strewn with gold leaf, complete the cake's truly royal decoration.

INGREDIENTS

For the cake

⅔ cup (100g) all-purpose flour
⅓ cup (45g) cocoa powder
½ tsp baking powder
⅛ tsp salt
4 eggs
⅔ cup (150g) superfine sugar
1 tsp vanilla extract
3 tbsp unsalted butter

For the frosting

5oz (150g) semisweet chocolate
3 eggs, separated
6 tbsp (90g) unsalted butter, at room temperature
1½ tsp vanilla extract
pinch of salt

For the filling and decoration

⅔ cup (150ml) heavy cream
1 tbsp superfine sugar
semisweet chocolate waves (see page 44)
edible gold leaf (optional)

1 Sift the flour, cocoa, baking powder, and salt together three times. Set aside.

2 Break the eggs into a large heatproof bowl, preferably a copper one, and gradually beat in the sugar, using a hand-held electric beater. Set the bowl over hot water and beat for 6–8 minutes, until the mixture has doubled in volume and is thick enough to leave a ribbon trail. Whisk in the vanilla.

3 Melt the butter and set aside. Sift the dry ingredients over the egg mixture, a third at a time, folding in each batch carefully. Fold in the butter.

4 Pour the mixture into the prepared pan and bake in the preheated oven for 35–40 minutes, or until the top of the cake springs back when lightly pressed. Leave the cake in the pan for a few minutes before turning it out onto a wire rack to cool.

5 For the frosting, melt the chocolate in a medium-size bowl (see page 33). While the chocolate is still hot, beat in the egg yolks, one by one. Cut the butter into small pieces and blend into the chocolate mixture. Stir in 1 teaspoon of the vanilla. Whisk the egg whites with the salt until stiff.

Oven temperature
350°F/180°C

Baking time
35–40 minutes

Baking pan
9in (23cm) springform pan, greased, lined, then greased and floured

Makes
8–10 slices

Storage
Keeps for 2–3 days in the refrigerator

Freezing
2 months, unfilled and undecorated

Step ahead
Make the cake; keeps for 2 days, wrapped, in the refrigerator

A rich egg-based frosting covers the cake

6 Fold a large spoonful of the whites into the chocolate mixture to lighten it. Carefully fold in the remaining whites.

7 For the filling, whip the cream to soft peaks, then fold in the sugar and remaining vanilla extract.

TO FINISH THE CAKE
1 Cut the cake into three layers (see page 50). Put the bottom layer on a thin cake board or flat plate and spread it with a third of the frosting. Add a second cake layer and spread it with the cream. Top with the remaining cake layer.

2 Cover the top and sides of the cake with the remaining chocolate frosting. Decorate with chocolate waves and edible gold leaf, if desired.

Touches of gold glitter on top of the chocolate

GATEAU ROYALE
Imaginatively decorated, this airy cake provides a sparkling finale for a celebratory occasion.

Devil's Food Cake

This rich cake, its frosting flavored with fruit juices, is an American classic.

INGREDIENTS

For the cake

3oz (90g) semisweet chocolate, chopped (see page 32)
1 tsp baking soda
2¼ cups (273g) self-rising cake flour
½ tsp salt
1 cup (250g) unsalted butter, softened
2½ cups (400g) packed, dark brown sugar
2 tsp vanilla extract
3 eggs
½ cup (125ml) buttermilk
1 cup (250ml) boiling water

For the frosting

1¼ cups (300g) superfine sugar
2 egg whites
1 tbsp lemon juice
3 tbsp frozen orange juice concentrate

1 Melt the chocolate (see page 33) and set aside.

2 Sift together the baking soda, flour, and salt and set aside.

3 Cream the butter until soft, add the sugar, and continue to beat until light and fluffy. Stir in the vanilla extract. Beat in the eggs, one at a time, adding a little flour if the mixture starts to curdle. Stir in the chocolate.

4 Fold in the dry ingredients, a third at a time, alternating with the buttermilk. Slowly stir in the boiling water.

5 Divide the mixture evenly between the prepared pans and put them in the preheated oven so they are not directly above each other. Bake for 30 minutes, or until the tops spring back when lightly touched.

6 Cool the cakes in the pans for 5 minutes before turning out onto wire racks to cool.

7 For the frosting, put all the ingredients in the top of a double boiler or in a bowl set over simmering water. Whisk until the mixture thickens and forms soft peaks. Remove from the heat and continue to beat until it is the right consistency for spreading (it should coat the back of a spoon).

8 Sandwich the cake layers with some of the frosting and spread the rest roughly over the top and sides of the cake with a narrow spatula.

Oven temperature
375°F/190°C

Baking time
30 minutes

Baking pans
Two 9in (23cm) shallow cake pans, greased and lined on the bottom

Makes
12–16 slices

Storage
Keeps for 2 days in the refrigerator

Freezing
1 month, unfrosted

White Chocolate Cake

INGREDIENTS

For the cake

1/4 cup (100g) all-purpose flour
6 tbsp (45g) cocoa powder
1/2 tsp baking powder
1/8 tsp salt
4 eggs
1/2 cup (150g) superfine sugar
1 tsp vanilla extract
3 tbsp unsalted butter

For the white chocolate buttercream

1 egg
1/3 cup (90g) granulated sugar
1/4 cup (50 ml) water
good pinch of cream of tartar
12 tbsp (180g) unsalted butter, at room temperature
8oz (250g) white chocolate
4 tbsp water

For the raspberry syrup

1/2 cup (125ml) raspberry preserves
4 tbsp framboise (raspberry liqueur)
white chocolate curls, to decorate (see page 43)

A plain chocolate sponge cake layered with a lightly alcoholic raspberry syrup and a rich white chocolate buttercream is the perfect choice for the lover of white chocolate.

White chocolate curls sit on white buttercream on this elegant cake

1 Sift the flour, cocoa, baking powder, and salt together three times. Set aside.

2 Break the eggs into a large heatproof bowl, preferably a copper one, and gradually beat in the sugar, using a hand-held electric beater. Set the bowl over hot water and beat for 6–8 minutes, until the mixture has doubled in volume and is thick enough to leave a ribbon trail when the whisk is lifted. Whisk in the vanilla.

3 Melt the butter over low heat and set aside. Sift the dry ingredients over the egg mixture, a third at a time, folding in each batch carefully with a large metal spoon. Fold in the melted butter.

4 Pour the mixture into the prepared pan and bake in the preheated oven for 35–40 minutes, or until the cake springs back when lightly pressed. Let the cake rest in the pan for a few minutes. Slip a knife around the inside of the pan to loosen the cake and turn out onto a wire rack to cool.

5 For the buttercream, beat the egg until pale and thick and set aside.

6 Put the sugar, water, and cream of tartar in a small saucepan. Dissolve the sugar over low heat, then boil until the syrup reaches 240°F (115°C) on a candy thermometer. Gradually pour the hot sugar syrup onto the egg, beating constantly. Continue beating until the mixture has cooled to room temperature.

7 Cut the butter into small pieces and beat them, a few at a time, into the egg mixture. Melt the white chocolate with the water (see page 34). When it has cooled to lukewarm, stir it into the buttercream.

8 For the syrup, sieve the raspberry preserves and stir in the liqueur.

TO FINISH THE CAKE

1 Cut the cake into three layers (see page 50). Place the top layer, upside down, on a thin round cake board or flat plate. Brush with half the raspberry syrup. Spread with a quarter of the buttercream.

2 Place the second layer on top. Brush with the remaining syrup and spread with another quarter of the cream. Place the third layer on top and cover the top and sides of the cake with the remaining buttercream. Decorate the cake with large white chocolate curls.

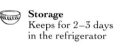

Oven temperature
350°F/180°C

Baking time
35–40 minutes

Baking pan
9in (23cm) springform pan, greased, lined, then greased and floured

Makes
8–10 slices

Storage
Keeps for 2–3 days in the refrigerator

Freezing
2–3 months

Mocha Roulade

This is an astonishingly light and delectable flourless chocolate roulade. I have filled it with a coffee cream, but it could be filled with plain or vanilla-flavored whipped cream. It is usual for it to crack as it is rolled up – a sign of its lightness.

INGREDIENTS

For the cake

4oz (125g) semisweet chocolate
2oz (60g) bittersweet chocolate
3 tbsp water
2 tbsp brandy
5 eggs, separated
¾ cup (180g) superfine sugar
pinch of salt

For the filling and decoration

1 tsp instant espresso coffee powder
1 tbsp boiling water
1¼ cups (300ml) heavy cream
1 tsp superfine sugar
semisweet chocolate triangles (see page 44)

1 Melt both chocolates, water, and brandy together (see page 34) and set aside to cool.

2 Whisk the egg yolks with the sugar until pale in color. Fold in the melted chocolate. Whisk the egg whites with the salt until stiff. Fold a spoonful of the whites into the yolks to lighten the mixture, then gently fold in the remaining whites.

3 Pour the mixture evenly into the prepared pan. Bake in the preheated oven for 15 minutes. Remove from the oven, cover with waxed paper and a damp cloth, and leave for several hours, or overnight.

4 For the filling, dissolve the coffee in the water. Whip the cream to soft peaks, then fold in the coffee and sugar.

5 Turn the roulade out onto a sheet of waxed paper dusted with confectioners' sugar. Peel off the lining paper (see step 1, below).

6 Put 3–4 tablespoons of the filling into a nylon pastry bag with a ½in (1cm) nozzle. Spread the remainder over the roulade. Roll up the long side of the roulade, using the sugared paper to help (see steps 2–3, below). Discard the paper.

7 Pipe the reserved filling on top of the roulade (see page 48) and set the chocolate triangles in it. Chill the roulade for several hours before serving.

VARIATION
This roulade makes an excellent Christmas Log. Decorate it with chocolate holly leaves cut from melted chocolate or from chocolate marzipan (see pages 44 and 76) and a red berry fruit.

Oven temperature
350°F/180°C

Baking time
15 minutes

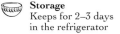
Baking pan
14 x 10 x ½in (36 x 25 x 1cm) jelly roll pan, greased and lined with baking parchment

Makes
12–16 slices

Storage
Keeps for 2–3 days in the refrigerator

How to make a roulade

1 To take the lining paper off the cold roulade, carefully lift the paper's front corners and peel it back toward you.

2 Use a narrow spatula to spread the filling, being careful not to take it right to the edges of the roulade.

3 To prevent the roulade from cracking deeply or the filling from pushing out, roll it up lightly, without pressing on it.

Coffee cream filling gives the roulade an extra piquancy

Chocolate Almond and Raspberry Roulade

An easy-to-roll sponge cake made with almonds is the basis of this roulade. It is filled with a luscious dark chocolate cream.

INGREDIENTS

For the cake

¼ cup (100g) almonds
½ cup (100g) superfine sugar
3 eggs
3 egg whites
pinch of salt
¼ cup (30g) all-purpose flour
2 tbsp unsalted butter, melted

For the raspberry syrup

¼ cup (75g) superfine sugar
⅓ cup (90ml) water
3 tbsp framboise (raspberry liqueur)

For the filling and decoration

4oz (125g) bittersweet chocolate
4oz (125g) semisweet chocolate
½ cup (125ml) milk
1 cup (250ml) heavy cream
1 pint (500g) fresh raspberries
chocolate leaves (see page 43)

Mocha Roulade combines coffee and chocolate in delicious style

1 Grind the almonds with 2 tablespoons of the sugar in a food processor or blender. Set aside 2 more tablespoons of sugar. Place the ground almonds and the remaining sugar in a large bowl. Add the eggs, one at a time, beating each egg until it is light and thick before adding the next.

2 Whisk the egg whites with the salt until stiff. Add the 2 tablespoons of sugar and whisk for 20 seconds

more, until glossy. Sift the flour over the almond mixture and carefully fold it in, using a large metal spoon. Fold in the whisked egg whites, a third at a time, and then the melted butter.

3 Turn the mixture into the prepared pan and spread it level. Bake in the preheated oven for 12–15 minutes, or until just firm. Remove the cake with its paper to a flat surface and leave until it is cool.

4 For the syrup, dissolve the sugar in the water over moderate heat, then boil until the syrup is clear. When it has cooled, add the framboise.

5 For the filling, melt the chocolates and milk together (see page 34). Whip the cream until it forms soft peaks. When the chocolate is tepid, fold in a large spoonful of cream. Fold the chocolate into the rest of the cream with a large metal spoon.

TO FINISH THE ROULADE

1 Turn the cake over onto a piece of baking parchment or waxed paper and carefully peel off the lining paper (see step 1, below left). Brush the surface with the syrup. Spread with two-thirds of the chocolate cream (see step 2, below left).

2 Set aside about 12 raspberries for decoration and scatter the rest over the chocolate cream.

3 Roll up the cake from the short side, using the paper to help. Spread the remaining chocolate cream over the top and sides of the roulade. Decorate with chocolate leaves and the reserved raspberries. Keep the roulade in the refrigerator, bringing it out an hour before serving, to allow it to come to room temperature.

Oven temperature
400°F/200°C

Baking time
12–15 minutes

Baking pan
15½ x 10½ x ½in (39 x 26 x 1cm) jelly roll pan, greased and lined with greased baking parchment

Makes
8–10 slices

Storage
Keeps for 2–3 days in the refrigerator

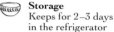

Marjolaine

An elegant example of Continental patisserie, this is a meringue, made with almonds and layered with an apricot filling and a smooth chocolate buttercream.

INGREDIENTS

For the cake

¼ cup (100g) almonds
½ cup (100g) sugar
3 eggs
3 egg whites
pinch of salt
¼ cup (30g) all-purpose flour
2 tbsp butter, melted

For the apricot filling

4 tbsp cold water
¼ tsp unflavored gelatin
⅓ cup (90g) dried apricots
½ cup (125ml) heavy cream
2 tbsp granulated sugar

For the buttercream

3 egg yolks
⅓ cup (90g) superfine sugar
⅓ cup (75ml) water
14 tbsp (200g) unsalted butter, softened
3½oz (100g) bittersweet chocolate, melted (see page 33)
cocoa powder, to decorate

1 For the cake, grind the almonds with 2 tablespoons of the sugar in a food processor or blender. Set aside 2 more tablespoons of sugar. Put the ground almonds and remaining sugar in a large bowl. Add the eggs, one at a time, beating each egg until it is light and thick before adding the next.

2 Whisk the egg whites with the salt until stiff. Add the 2 tablespoons of sugar and whisk for 20 seconds more, until glossy. Sift the flour over the almond mixture and carefully fold in, using a large metal spoon. Fold in the egg whites, a third at a time, then the melted butter.

3 Turn the mixture into the prepared pan and spread it level. Bake in a preheated oven for 12–15 minutes, or just until firm. Remove the cake with its paper to a flat surface to cool.

4 For the apricot filling, measure the water into a cup, sprinkle over the gelatin, and leave until spongy. Put the cup in a bowl of hot water to dissolve the gelatin. Put the apricots, cream, and sugar in a saucepan and simmer for 10 minutes. Stir in the gelatin. Purée in a food processor or blender and let cool at room temperature.

5 For the buttercream, beat the egg yolks together in a bowl. Gently heat the sugar and water together until the sugar has dissolved, bring to a boil, and boil until the syrup reaches the soft ball stage, 240°F (115°C) on a candy thermometer.

6 Gradually pour the syrup over the eggs, beating constantly, until the mixture is cool and thick. Cream the butter and blend into the egg mixture. Mix in the melted chocolate.

TO FINISH THE CAKE

1 Turn the cake over onto a piece of waxed paper and remove the lining paper. Cut the cake into four equal-size rectangles.

2 Put one rectangle on a thin cake board or flat cake plate and spread with a quarter of the buttercream. Add a second layer and spread on the apricot filling. Add the third layer and spread it with buttercream. Put the last rectangle on top and cover the sides and top with the remaining buttercream.

3 Chill the Marjolaine until firm. Remove from the refrigerator 1 hour before serving. To decorate, sift a layer of cocoa over the top and score with a knife. Serve the cake in slices, cut with a hot, dry knife.

Oven temperature
400°F/200°C

Baking time
12–15 minutes

Baking pan
14 x 10 x ½in (36 x 25 x 1cm) jelly roll pan, lined with buttered waxed paper

Makes
12–16 slices

Storage
Keeps for 2–3 days in the refrigerator

Marble Pound Cake

Equal weights of butter, flour, sugar, and eggs have been the formula for pound cakes for centuries. The buttery taste of this chocolate version makes it the perfect choice for serving with tea or coffee.

INGREDIENTS

1 cup (125g) potato flour
1 cup (125g) all-purpose flour
1 tsp baking powder
¼ tsp salt
1 cup (250g) unsalted butter, softened
1 cup (250g) superfine sugar
4 eggs
2 tbsp milk
1 tsp vanilla extract
3oz (90g) semisweet chocolate, melted
2 tbsp cocoa powder blended with 2 tbsp boiling water
½ quantity Chocolate Glaze, to decorate (see page 136)

1 Sift the flours, baking powder, and salt together twice and set aside.

2 Cream the butter and sugar until light and fluffy. Mix the eggs with the milk and vanilla and add very gradually to the butter mixture. Fold in the flour, a quarter at a time.

3 Spoon half the mixture into the prepared mold. Mix the melted chocolate and cocoa into the remaining mixture and spoon into the mold, swirling the mixture for a marbled effect.

4 Bake the cake in the preheated oven for 1 hour, or until firm. Leave it in the mold for 10 minutes, then turn out onto a wire rack to cool.

5 Put the cooled cake on a piece of waxed paper. When the Chocolate Glaze has cooled to a coating consistency (it should coat the back of a spoon), pour it over the top of the cake, letting it drip down the sides. Leave until set.

Oven temperature
350°F/180°C

Baking time
1 hour

Baking pan
Large tubular cake pan, greased with melted butter and floured

Makes
12 slices

Storage
Keeps for 2–3 days in the refrigerator

Freezing
1 month

Dacquoise

This is a wonderful confection of hazelnut meringues layered with chocolate cream and topped with raspberries or strawberries. It can easily be transformed into a summer dessert by replacing the chocolate with whipped cream, mixed with fresh berry fruits.

INGREDIENTS

For the meringues

2 cups (250g) hazelnuts, toasted and skinned (see page 38)
1 tbsp cornstarch
1¼ cups (300g) superfine sugar
2 tbsp cocoa powder
6 egg whites

For the filling and decoration

1 quantity Chocolate Ganache (see page 136)
1 pint (400g) strawberries

1 Finely grind the cooled nuts in a food processor with the cornstarch and 3 tablespoons of the sugar. Tip the mixture into a bowl and stir in the cocoa.

2 Whisk 3 of the egg whites to form soft peaks. Gradually whisk in half the remaining sugar to form stiff glossy peaks. Fold in half the nut mixture.

3 Divide the mixture between the prepared baking sheets and spread out in the marked circles. Bake in the preheated oven for 1 hour, or until crisp and dry. Cool on wire racks.

4 Reline the baking sheets. Make up the remaining meringue ingredients and bake two more disks. When they are cold, peel off the lining papers.

5 Make the Chocolate Ganache, whisking until it is fluffy and cool.

6 Put a meringue disk on a serving plate and spread with Chocolate Ganache. Repeat with the other disks, spreading the top one with all the remaining cream. Chill for 2 hours. Arrange the fresh strawberries over the top of the Dacquoise before serving.

Oven temperature
275°F/140°C

Baking time
1 hour per batch

Baking pans
Two flat baking sheets, each lined with baking parchment or foil and marked with a 9in (23cm) circle

Makes
12 slices

Storage
Keeps for 2–3 days in the refrigerator

Wedding Cake

This rich chocolate sponge cake, iced and decorated with white chocolate, will please all chocolate lovers. Each of the three cakes is cut into layers, which are then sandwiched together with a buttercream flavored with fresh strawberries. The combination of flavors is delicious. The sponge cakes freeze well and can be thawed out overnight at room temperature. The individually iced cakes can be assembled and decorated the day before the wedding and stored in a cool place.

The Wedding Cake slices easily and will serve up to 100 guests

INGREDIENTS

For the 12in (30cm) cake

9oz (275g) bittersweet chocolate

5oz (150g) semisweet chocolate

1 cup (225ml) water

12 eggs

1½ cups (375g) superfine sugar

2⅓ cups (290g) all-purpose flour

For the 9in (23cm) cake

8oz (250g) bittersweet chocolate

2oz (60g) semisweet chocolate

½ cup (125ml) water

7 eggs

¾ cup (200g) superfine sugar

1¼ cups (150g) all-purpose flour

For the 6in (15cm) cake

5oz (150g) bittersweet chocolate

6 tbsp (90 ml) water

5 eggs

½ cup (150g) superfine sugar

1 cup (125g) all-purpose flour

For the buttercream

18 egg yolks

3 cups (625g) superfine sugar

1½ cups (350ml) water

6 cups (1.5kg) unsalted butter, softened

½ pint (250g) strawberries

For the white chocolate icing

2¼lb (1.15kg) white chocolate, chopped into small pieces

1¾ cups (400ml) heavy cream

For the white chocolate decoration

white chocolate ribbons and cutout petals (see pages 44 and 45), made with 1½lb (750g) white chocolate

Make the 12in (30cm) cake first, then make the 9in (23cm) and 6in (15cm) cakes together.

1 For each cake, put the chocolate and water in a small saucepan and slowly bring to a boil. Remove from the heat, stir until blended, and let cool.

2 Break the eggs into a large (very large for the 12-egg cake) heatproof bowl and set it over a pan of hot but not boiling water. Using an electric hand-held beater, whisk the eggs with the sugar until the mixture has doubled in volume and is thick enough to leave a ribbon trail, about 25 minutes for the 12-egg cake, 12 minutes for the 7-egg cake, and 10 minutes for the 5-egg cake.

3 Sift the flour over the egg mixture, a third at a time, folding it in carefully. Fold in the melted chocolate.

4 Pour into the prepared pan and bake in the preheated oven for the recommended time, or until a skewer inserted in the center comes out clean. Leave the cake in the pan for a few minutes, then turn out onto a wire rack to cool.

5 For the buttercream, put the egg yolks in a large bowl and whisk until they are pale and thick. Put the sugar and water in a heavy-based saucepan. Simmer, covered, for 1 minute to dissolve the sugar. Uncover and boil until the syrup reaches 240°F (115°C) on a candy thermometer. Gradually pour the hot sugar syrup onto the eggs (avoiding the beaters), beating constantly. Continue beating until the mixture has cooled to room temperature.

6 Cut the softened butter into small pieces and beat them into the mixture, a few at a time. Set aside a third of the buttercream. Mash the strawberries and beat them into the remaining buttercream.

7 Slice each cake into three layers. Use the strawberry buttercream to sandwich the layers together. Put each cake on the appropriate-size thin cake board and set each one on a wire rack with a large square of foil underneath.

Oven temperature
350°F/180°C

Baking time
60–65 minutes for the 12in (30cm) cake; 40–45 minutes for the 9in (23cm) cake; 35–40 minutes for the 6in (15cm) cake

Baking pans
12 x 2in (30 x 5cm) cake pan; 9 x 2in (23 x 5cm) cake pan; 6 x 2in (15 x 5cm) cake pan, each greased, lined on the bottom with waxed paper, then greased again and floured

To assemble the cake
14in (35.5cm) heavy cake board; 12in (30cm) thin cake board; 9in (23cm) thin cake board; 6in (15cm) thin cake board
6 acrylic cake skewers
3¼ yds (3m) of 1in (2.5cm)-wide ribbon
4 yds (3½m) of ¾in (1.5cm)-wide ribbon
stainless steel pins

Makes
100 slices

Storage
Sponge cakes keep for 3 days in the refrigerator; iced cakes keep for 3 days in the refrigerator

Freezing
2 months, unfrosted and undecorated

8 Pour a thin layer of the plain buttercream over each cake, returning to the bowl any buttercream that runs onto the foil. Chill the cakes for a few minutes to set the buttercream.

9 For the icing, melt the white chocolate carefully (see page 33). Bring the cream to a simmer, remove from the heat and let cool, then stir it into the chocolate.

10 Cool the icing to a spreading consistency (it should coat the back of a spoon) and pour enough over each cake to cover it, spreading the icing over the top and down the sides with a narrow spatula. Also put a thin layer, about 1½in (3.5cm) wide, on the top edge of the heavy cake board. If the icing becomes too cold to spread, gently reheat it over hot water. Let the icing set.

TO ASSEMBLE THE CAKE

1 Push the acrylic skewers into the large cake, in an even circle about 1½in (3.5cm) in from the edge; mark the point where they are level with the top of the cake and remove them. Cut the skewers to the mark and put them back in the cake. Use the cut-off pieces of the skewers to make similar supports for the middle tier.

2 Leaving the cakes on their thin boards, set the large cake in the center of the heavy cake board, the middle-size cake on the large cake, and the small cake on top.

3 Pin the wide ribbon around the heavy cake board and the narrow ribbon around the bottom edge of each cake.

Ribbons disguise the seams between the Wedding Cake's three tiers

TO DECORATE THE CAKE

Assemble 9 bunches of chocolate ribbons and petals, each with 3 ribbons and 5 petals. Arrange 4 bunches on the bottom tier, 3 on the middle tier, and 2 on the top tier, holding the pieces in place with dabs of melted white chocolate made from the chocolate ribbon trimmings and spooned into a paper piping bag. Pleat pieces of the narrow ribbon and pin into the center of each bunch.

Chocolate and real ribbons give a fairy-tale quality to the Wedding Cake

Dessert Cakes

The single-layer cakes in this section make fine dessert cakes, especially good when served with a sauce, such as crème anglaise, or a fruit coulis or syrup, like the kumquat syrup made for the Celestial Kumquat Torte on this page. Many of the cakes here are in the rich tradition of the Austrian and German torte, often enriched with nuts or seeds and containing little or no flour. The classic Sacher Torte is among such cakes here, as well as two delicious Italian cakes, combining chocolate with chestnuts or amaretti cookies.

Celestial Kumquat Torte

Kumquats, a native of China introduced into the United States in about 1850, are closely related to citrus fruits but, uniquely, have a sweet edible rind. The sharp yet sweet flavor of poached kumquats and their syrup goes well with many chocolate desserts, including this rich torte.

INGREDIENTS

For the kumquats

1lb (500g) kumquats
½ cup (150g) granulated sugar
1¼ cups (300ml) water

For the cake

⅓ cup (45g) self-rising cake flour
½ cup (150g) superfine sugar
pinch of salt
3 eggs
3oz (90g) bittersweet chocolate
1 tbsp cocoa powder
7 tbsp (100g) unsalted butter

For the glaze

4oz (125g) semisweet chocolate
2 tbsp unsalted butter
2 tbsp milk
chocolate leaves, to decorate (see page 43)

1 Wash the kumquats and halve them lengthwise, leaving 9–10 whole for decoration. Put in a pan with the sugar and water. Bring to a boil and cook very slowly for 30 minutes, until soft. Set aside.

2 For the cake, put the flour, sugar, salt, and eggs in a large bowl set over hot but not boiling water and beat with an electric beater for 8 minutes. The mixture should become very thick and leave a ribbon trail when the beater is lifted.

3 Melt the chocolate, cocoa powder, and butter together (see page 34). Add to the egg mixture and beat for a few minutes. Pour the mixture into the prepared pan and bake in the preheated oven for 25 minutes, or until the cake is springy to the touch. Remove from the oven and run a knife around the inside edge of the pan. Leave for 10 minutes before turning out onto a wire rack.

4 Melt the glaze ingredients together (see page 34). Put the cake, on the wire rack, on a plate to catch excess glaze. Cool the glaze slightly so it thickens, then pour it over the warm cake, spreading it evenly with a narrow spatula (see page 49). Leave for 10 minutes to set.

5 Decorate the top with chocolate leaves and the whole kumquats and serve the cake lukewarm, with the remaining kumquats and syrup.

Oven temperature
325°F/160°C

Baking time
25 minutes

Baking pan
8in (20cm) springform pan, greased and lined on the bottom

Makes
8–10 slices

Storage
Keeps for 2–3 days in the refrigerator

Chocolate Hazelnut Cake

Crunchy hazelnuts help give this cake an excellent texture and flavor. Because it cuts well, the cake is a good choice for lunch boxes and picnic baskets. It is also good served with whipped cream.

INGREDIENTS

For the cake

¼ cup (90g) hazelnuts, toasted and skinned (see page 38)

½ cup (140g) superfine sugar

3oz (90g) bittersweet chocolate, chopped (see page 32)

3oz (90g) semisweet chocolate, chopped (see page 32)

12 tbsp (180g) unsalted butter, cut into small pieces

4 eggs, separated

1 tsp vanilla extract

¼ cup (30g) all-purpose flour

¼ tsp salt

¼ tsp cream of tartar

For the decoration

1 quantity Chocolate Glaze (see page 136)

1oz (30g) white chocolate

1oz (30g) milk chocolate

1 Grind the hazelnuts with 2 tablespoons of the sugar. Melt both chocolates with the butter (see page 34). Set aside.

2 Whisk the egg yolks with ⅓ cup (90g) of the sugar until pale and thick. Stir in the warm chocolate mixture and the vanilla. Mix the flour and salt with the hazelnuts and fold into the chocolate mixture.

3 Beat the egg whites with the cream of tartar until they form soft peaks. Add the remaining sugar and continue to beat until the whites are stiff.

4 Using a large metal spoon, fold a spoonful of the whites into the chocolate mixture to lighten it. Carefully fold in the remaining whites. Scrape the mixture into the prepared pan and bake in the preheated oven for 35–40 minutes; the center should still be moist. Cool the cake in the pan on a wire rack. Press the top level and turn out onto a thin cake board.

5 Make the Chocolate Glaze. Spread a quarter of the glaze over the cake to keep the crumbs in place. Chill until set. Cover with the remaining glaze (see page 49). The glaze may need warming over hot water first.

6 Melt the white and milk chocolates for decoration separately and spoon them into paper piping bags.

7 Pipe circles of the two chocolates alternately on the cake and feather them with a skewer (see page 47).

 Oven temperature
375°F/190°C

Baking time
35–40 minutes

Baking pan
9in (23cm) springform pan, greased and lined on the bottom

Makes
10–12 slices

Storage
Keeps for 3–4 days in the refrigerator

Freezing
1–2 months

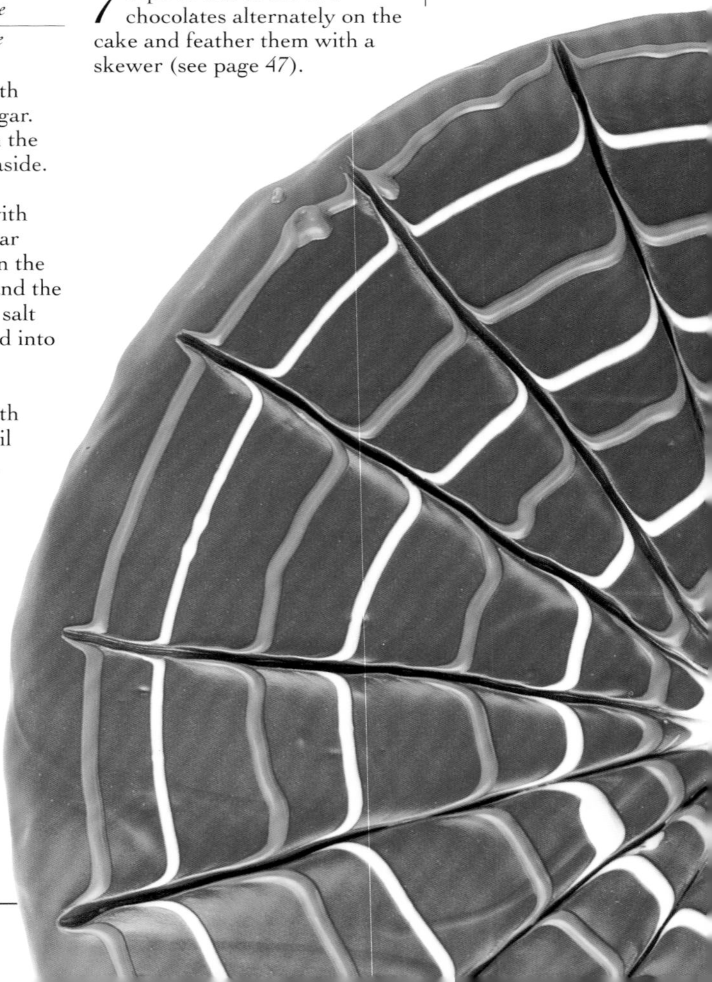

Chocolate Truffle Cake

INGREDIENTS

For the crust

5 cups (180g) graham
crackers, crushed

2 tbsp cocoa powder,
sifted

2 tbsp light brown sugar

5 tbsp (75g) unsalted butter, melted

For the filling and decoration

8oz (250g) semisweet chocolate

3oz (90g) bittersweet chocolate

2½ cups (600ml) heavy cream

2 tbsp milk

2 tbsp brandy or rum or
1 tsp vanilla extract

cocoa powder

white and semisweet chocolate piped
curves (see page 47)

*A combination of
melted chocolate and
whipped cream creates this
mousse-like cake, popular
with today's restaurant
chefs. This version has a
chocolate crust for added
texture and crunch.*

1 Mix together the crushed cookies, cocoa, brown sugar, and melted butter. Press in an even layer on the prepared pan's base. Bake in the preheated oven for 10 minutes.

Carefully remove the side of the pan and put the base, with the crust on it, on a wire rack to cool. When it is cool, reassemble the pan.

2 For the filling, melt the chocolates together (see page 33) and let stand until the mixture has cooled to tepid. It should still be liquid.

3 Set the cream in its container in a bowl of hot water until it is cool but no longer refrigerator cold.

4 Whisk the cream with the milk and brandy or vanilla until it is thick enough to leave a ribbon trail when the whisk is lifted. Be careful not to over-whip the cream.

5 Blend a spoonful of the cream into the tepid chocolate, then quickly fold the chocolate into the rest of the cream, using a large metal spoon. Pour the mixture over the crust in the pan and smooth the top with a narrow spatula. Cover the pan with plastic wrap. Chill for at least 4 hours, preferably overnight.

6 Remove the cake from the pan and leave it at room temperature for 30 minutes before serving.

7 Just before you serve the cake, sift a fine layer of cocoa powder over the top. Decorate with the white and semisweet chocolate piped curves.

Oven temperature
350°F/180°C

Baking time
10 minutes for
the crust

Baking pan
10in (25cm)
springform pan

Makes
10–12 slices

Storage
Keeps for 3–4 days
in the refrigerator

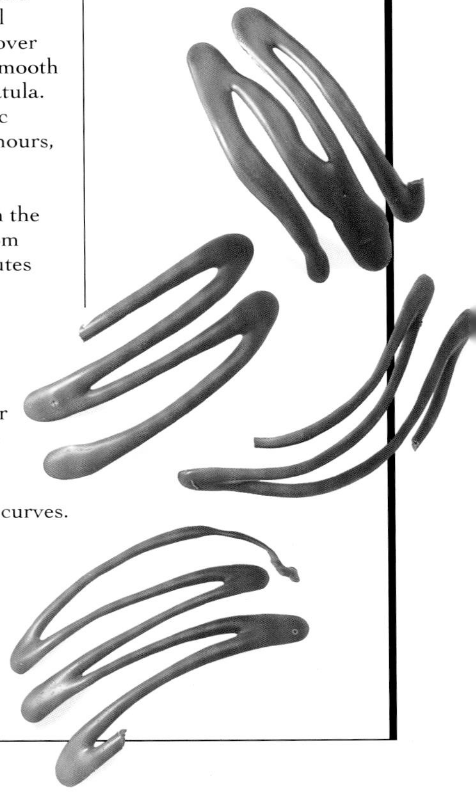

Sacher Torte

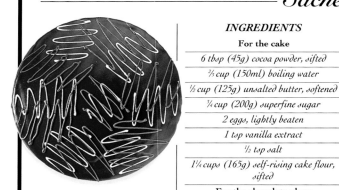

This famous cake, the original ingredients of which are still a closely guarded secret, was created in 1832 by the Austrian chef Franz Sacher for Prince Metternich. Later in the century, it was the subject of a seven-year legal battle over the ownership of its name. This version has a delicate chocolate flavor and a firm dark chocolate icing.

INGREDIENTS

For the cake

6 tbsp (45g) cocoa powder, sifted
⅔ cup (150ml) boiling water
½ cup (125g) unsalted butter, softened
¼ cup (200g) superfine sugar
2 eggs, lightly beaten
1 tsp vanilla extract
½ tsp salt
1¼ cups (165g) self-rising cake flour, sifted

For the chocolate glaze

½ cup (125g) unsalted butter
3oz (90g) bittersweet chocolate
3oz (90g) semisweet chocolate
1 tbsp corn syrup

For the decoration

1oz (30g) white chocolate
1oz (30g) milk chocolate

1 For the cake, whisk the sifted cocoa and water together until smooth. Set aside to cool to room temperature.

2 Beat the butter and sugar together until light and fluffy. Gradually add the eggs and vanilla. If the mixture threatens to curdle, stir in a tablespoon of the flour. Stir in the cocoa mixture and salt.

3 Sift the flour over the mixture, a third at a time, folding in each part carefully with a large metal spoon before adding the next.

4 Scrape the mixture into the prepared pan and bake in the preheated oven for 35–40 minutes, until a skewer inserted in the center comes out clean.

5 Let the cake cool in the pan for 5 minutes, then turn it out onto a wire rack.

6 Melt the ingredients for the chocolate glaze together (see page 34). Set the cake, on the wire rack, on a flat plate and pour the glaze over the top and sides, using a narrow spatula to spread it (see page 49).

7 For the decoration, melt the white and milk chocolates separately and spoon into paper piping bags (see page 46). Pipe zigzag lines of the chocolates over the top of the cake. Chill the cake to set the decoration.

Oven temperature
350°F/180°C

Baking time
35–40 minutes

Baking pan
9in (23cm) springform pan, greased, floured, and lined on the bottom

Makes
10–12 slices

Storage
Keeps for 3–4 days in the refrigerator

Freezing
1–2 months

Le Diabolo

More dessert than cake, this is very luscious and richly chocolate-flavored – an ultimate confection. To savor its full flavor and melting texture, serve it at room temperature, with a bowl of thick whipped cream on the side.

INGREDIENTS

6oz (180g) semisweet or bittersweet chocolate, chopped (see page 33)

12 tbsp (180g) unsalted butter, cut into small pieces

2 tsp vanilla extract

4 eggs, separated

½ cup (140g) superfine sugar

½ cup (60g) ground almonds

¼ cup (30g) all-purpose flour, sifted

⅛ tsp salt

⅛ tsp cream of tartar

For the decoration

cocoa powder

confectioners' sugar

chocolate leaves (see page 43)

1 Melt the chocolate and butter together (see page 34) and stir in the vanilla.

2 Whisk the egg yolks with ⅓ cup (90g) of the sugar until pale and thick. Stir in the warm chocolate mixture, then the almonds, flour, and salt.

3 Beat the egg whites with the cream of tartar until they form soft peaks. Add the remaining sugar and continue to beat until the whites are stiff.

4 Fold a large spoonful of the whites into the chocolate mixture to lighten it. Carefully fold in the remaining whites.

5 Scrape the mixture into the prepared pan and bake in the preheated oven for 40 minutes, or until a skewer inserted in the center of the cake shows moist crumbs. Leave the cake in the pan on a wire rack to cool. Press the cake level before removing it from the pan.

6 To decorate the cake, dust the top with cocoa. Put leaves on the cocoa and dust the confectioners' sugar around them. Lift off the leaves. Arrange chocolate leaves on top so that the leaf shapes, stenciled in confectioners' sugar, also show.

Oven temperature
375°F/190°C

Baking time
40 minutes

Baking pan
8in (20cm) springform pan, greased and lined

Makes
10–12 slices

Storage
Keeps for 3–4 days in the refrigerator

Amaretti Chocolate Cake

Amaretti cookies, which have a strong almond flavor, provide the distinctive taste in this Italian chocolate cake. As it bakes, the cake separates into two layers, with the amaretti crumbs settling in the lower half of the cake.

INGREDIENTS

12 tbsp (180g) unsalted butter

½ cup (150g) superfine sugar

4 eggs, separated

¼ cup (90g) self-rising flour, sifted

pinch of salt

1½ cups (90g) crushed amaretti cookies

½ cup (125ml) whole milk

2oz (60g) bittersweet chocolate, finely grated (see page 42)

pinch of cream of tartar

confectioners' sugar, to decorate

1 Cream the butter and sugar until light and fluffy. Add the egg yolks, one at a time, beating well after each addition.

2 Mix together the flour, salt, and cookies. Fold into the butter and egg mixture, a little at a time, alternating with the milk. Add the grated chocolate.

3 Whisk the egg whites with the cream of tartar until they form stiff peaks. Fold a large spoonful of the whites into the cake mixture to lighten it, then carefully fold in the remaining egg whites.

4 Pour the mixture into the prepared pan and bake in the preheated oven for 45 minutes, or until a skewer inserted in the center comes out clean. Cool the cake on a wire rack. Remove from the pan and dust with sifted confectioners' sugar.

Oven temperature
350°F/180°C

Baking time
45 minutes

Baking pan
9in (23cm) springform pan, greased, lined, then greased and floured

Makes
8–10 slices

Storage
Keeps for 4–5 days in the refrigerator

Torta di Castagne e Cioccolato

This classic Italian recipe, somewhere between a dessert and a cake, is sold in cake and confectionery shops in many parts of Italy. Serve it at room temperature with a bowl of crème fraîche or creamy mascarpone and a pitcher of chocolate sauce.

INGREDIENTS

12oz (375g) fresh chestnuts, cooked and peeled, or canned
⅔ cup (150ml) milk
1 cup (250g) superfine sugar
5 eggs, separated
7 tbsp (100g) unsalted butter, softened
2 tsp vanilla extract
¼ tsp salt
3½oz (100g) bittersweet chocolate
½ cup (100g) almonds
zest of 1 lemon, grated
pinch of cream of tartar
confectioners' sugar, to decorate

1 Put the chestnuts and milk in a saucepan, cover, and slowly bring to a boil. Remove from the heat and set aside to cool.

2 Set 3 tablespoons of the sugar aside. In a large bowl, whisk the remaining sugar with the egg yolks. Blend in the softened butter, vanilla, and salt.

3 Put the chocolate and almonds in a food processor and process until finely grated.

Stir the chocolate and nuts into the egg mixture.

4 Purée the chestnuts with the milk in a food processor and mix into the egg mixture. Stir in the lemon zest.

5 Whisk the egg whites with the cream of tartar until they form soft peaks. Gradually add the reserved sugar and whisk for 20 seconds more, or until glossy. Fold a large spoonful of the whites into the cake mixture to lighten it, then carefully fold in the remaining whites.

6 Pour the mixture into the prepared pan and bake in the preheated oven for 50 minutes, or until a skewer inserted in the center comes out clean.

7 Set the cake on a wire rack, run a knife around the inside edge of the pan, and leave for 10 minutes. Invert onto a wire rack to cool. Sift the confectioners' sugar over the cake to serve, with a creamy cheese and a pitcher of chocolate sauce, if desired.

Oven temperature
350°F/180°C

Baking time
50 minutes

Baking pan
1½in (3.5cm)-deep 10in (25cm) cake pan, greased, lined on the bottom, then greased and floured

Makes
12–16 slices

Storage
Keeps for 2–3 days in the refrigerator

Striped Cheesecake

Although this cake looks as if it must be tricky to make, it could not be easier. By spooning the light and dark mixtures one on top of the other, the circles appear as if by magic. The cheesecake's fine texture comes from using a rich, creamy cream cheese.

INGREDIENTS

For the crust

3½ cups (225g) graham crackers, finely crushed
3 tbsp cocoa powder, sifted
2 tbsp light brown sugar
6 tbsp (90g) butter, melted

For the filling

1½lb (750g) cream cheese
1 cup (200g) superfine sugar
3 extra large eggs
5oz (150g) semisweet chocolate, melted with ¼ cup (50 ml) water (see page 34)
2 tsp vanilla extract

1 For the crust, put the crushed graham crackers in a bowl. Stir in the cocoa and

sugar. Pour over the melted butter and toss with a fork to blend. Press the crumbs evenly into the bottom of the springform pan. (If desired, reserve 3 or 4 tablespoonfuls of the crumbs to press around the side of the baked cheesecake.)

2 Bake in the preheated oven at the higher setting for 10 minutes. Cool on a wire rack. Reduce the oven temperature to the lower setting.

3 Carefully remove the side of the springform pan from the crust and lightly grease it with butter. When the crust has cooled, reassemble the springform pan.

Oven temperature
350°F/180°C; then 325°F/160°C

Baking time
10 minutes for the crust; 1 hour, 10 minutes for the cheesecake

Baking pan
9 x 2½in (23 x 6cm) springform pan, only sides greased

Makes
12–14 slices

Storage
Keeps for 1 week in the refrigerator

TO MAKE THE FILLING

1 Put the cream cheese in a large bowl. Beat, using a hand-held beater or an electric mixer, until smooth. Continue to mix, gradually adding the sugar. Add the eggs, one at a time, beating only enough to combine them with the rest of the mixture.

2 Pour about half the cheese mixture into another bowl and add the warm melted chocolate and water. Add 1 teaspoon of vanilla to both the light and chocolate mixtures.

3 Pour a little less than half of the light mixture into the center of the pan; tilt the pan so it spreads out in an even layer and covers the crust (see step 1, below). Gently pour a little less than half the chocolate mixture over the center of the light mixture and let it spread out, without tilting the pan (see step 2, below).

4 Alternate the layers, using about half the remaining

mixture each time, until both mixtures are used up, ending with the light mixture (see steps 3–4, below). You should get four pourings of the light mixture and three of the chocolate mixture.

5 Put a pan of hot water on the bottom rack of the preheated oven and the cheesecake on the rack above. Bake for 1 hour and 10 minutes, or until the light mixture in the center is just set. The chocolate mixture will firm up when cool.

6 Remove the cake from the oven and run a knife around the inside edge to release the cake. Set the cheesecake, in the pan, on a wire rack to cool.

7 Carefully remove the side of the pan. Chill the cheesecake until cold. Slide a narrow spatula between the bottom of the pan and the crust and remove the cheesecake to a serving plate. Leave the cheesecake at room temperature for an hour before serving.

Simple stripes make an impressive decoration for the cheesecake

How to make the cheesecake

1 *Pour about half the light mixture into the pan, tilting it a little to help the mixture spread over the crust.*

2 *Add the first chocolate stripe carefully in the center of the light layer. As it settles, it pushes the light layer outward.*

3 *Use a cup to pour in successive layers of mixture: this ensures that you have control over the amount added each time.*

4 *The final pouring should be of the light mixture. The pan will be filled to within 1in (2.5cm) of the top.*

The stripes go through the cheesecake

Valentine's Day Cake

What better way to express your love on Valentine's Day than to share this gorgeous, rose-decorated, heart-shaped chocolate cake with your beloved?

Roses and leaves molded from chocolate marzipan decorate the cake

INGREDIENTS

For the cake

1 quantity Le Diabolo (see page 73)

For the chocolate marzipan

2 tbsp cocoa powder

4–5 tsp boiling water

1¼lb (875g) white marzipan

For the decoration

3 tbsp apricot jam, melted with 1 tbsp water and sieved (apricot glaze)

4 chocolate marzipan roses (see page 48) and 14 leaves (see below)

2 yards (2m) of ½in (1cm)-wide ribbon

1 Make the Le Diabolo mixture and put it into the prepared pan. Bake in the preheated oven for about 1 hour, or until a skewer inserted in the center comes out clean.

2 Put the cake, in the pan, on a wire rack to cool completely. Remove the cake from the pan. Peel off the baking parchment.

3 For the chocolate marzipan, blend the cocoa with enough boiling water to make a smooth, stiff paste. Allow it to cool, then knead it into the marzipan until the marzipan is smoothly chocolate-colored throughout. If the marzipan is not to be used immediately, wrap it in plastic wrap and store in a cool place.

TO DECORATE THE CAKE

1 Put the cake on the cake board and brush it all over with the warm apricot glaze.

2 Set aside one-third of the marzipan. Roll out the rest on a surface lightly dusted with cocoa to a circular shape about 10½in (26cm) across.

3 Carefully pick up the marzipan, supported on the rolling pin, and lay it over the cake. Dust your fingers with a little cocoa and smooth the marzipan gently over the top and down the sides of the cake.

4 Trim the marzipan neatly around the bottom edge of the cake. Set the trimmings aside.

5 Take about two-thirds of the remaining piece of marzipan and roll it out very thin on a surface lightly dusted with cocoa to a size large enough to cover the top of the cakeboard.

6 Carefully lift the cake off the board and put it to one side. Using the rolling pin, lift the marzipan onto the board and smooth it over. Trim the marzipan around the top edge of the board. Keep the trimmings.

7 Spread a little apricot glaze over the center of the marzipan-covered board and put the cake back in place.

8 Knead together the leftover marzipan and trimmings. Use to make molded roses (see page 48) and leaves. To make marzipan leaves, press a small clean rose leaf onto thinly rolled-out marzipan, run a knife round the edge of the leaf, then lift it off the marzipan. Shape the leaf into a curve over your fingers. Put the roses and leaves in a warm, dry place to firm up (being made of marzipan, they will not become hard).

9 Arrange the roses and leaves on the cake, pressing them gently into place. Fix the ribbon around the bottom edge of the cake and around the edge of the cake board, using stainless-steel pins to secure it in place.

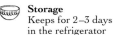

Oven temperature
350°F/180°C

Baking time
About 1 hour

Baking equipment
8in (20cm) heart-shaped cake pan, greased and lined with baking parchment; 10in (25cm) heart-shaped thick cake board

Makes
16–20 slices

Storage
Keeps for 2–3 days in the refrigerator

Step ahead
Make the apricot glaze a day ahead; make the chocolate marzipan a few hours beforehand

**VALENTINE'S DAY
CAKE** *There is double
chocolate enjoyment in this
romantic, rose-covered cake,
for beneath the rich chocolate
marzipan covering is a luscious
chocolate and almond cake.*

*Roses bring
true romance to
a special cake*

Snacktime Chocolate

Homemade squares and small cakes are always greatly appreciated, few more so than the Brownies that open this section. They are among the easiest of squares to bake, and there are many variations on the basic recipe. Other recipes here with the same virtues of being quick to make and delicious to eat are Chocolate Muffins and Bishop's Bread, a splendid chocolate tea bread. Other favorites here are the choux pastry treats, Eclairs and Profiteroles, and meringues have been given the full chocolate treatment, too.

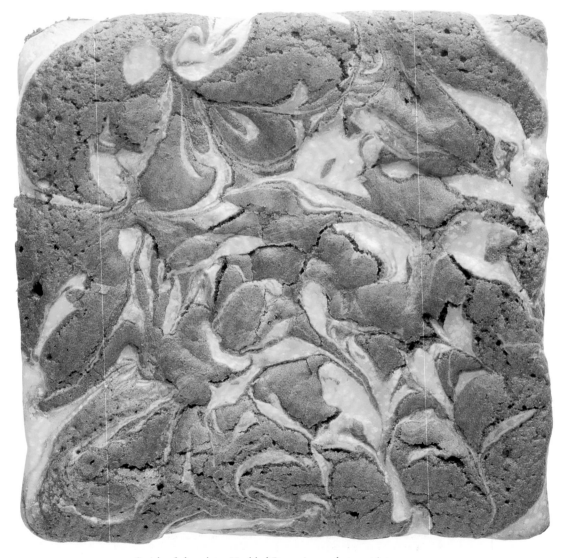

Swirls of chocolate: Marbled Brownies ready to cut into squares

Brownies

There must be hundreds of recipes for brownies, and this is one of the best. It has the added virtue of being quick to make. There is an easily made marbled variation, too, in which the walnuts are replaced by cream cheese.

INGREDIENTS

½ cup (125g) lightly salted butter
⅓ cup (45g) cocoa powder
2 eggs
1 cup (250g) superfine sugar
½ cup (60g) self-rising flour
¾ cup (90g) walnuts

1 Gently melt the butter in a small, heavy-based saucepan, then stir in the cocoa until blended and set aside.

2 Beat the eggs until light and fluffy. Gradually add the sugar and stir in the chocolate mixture. Sift the flour over the top and fold it into the mixture. Fold in the nuts.

3 Pour the mixture into the prepared pan and bake in the preheated oven for 30–35 minutes, or until just cooked through and springy to the touch. Brownies are at their best when moist, so be careful not to overbake them.

4 Cool the brownies in the pan. Turn it out and cut into squares. If desired, melt 2oz (60g) semisweet chocolate (see page 32) and spread over the cooled cake before cutting it into squares.

VARIATION
Marbled Brownies
For these, make the Brownies recipe to the end of step 2, replacing the walnuts with 1 teaspoon vanilla extract.

For the marbling, whisk together ¾ cup (180g) cream cheese, 1 egg, and ⅓ cup (90g) superfine sugar; sift ¼ cup (30g) self-rising flour over this mixture and fold in. Add 1 teaspoon vanilla extract.

Pour three-quarters of the basic brownie mixture into the prepared pan and spread the cream cheese mixture over it. Drop spoonfuls of the remaining brownie mixture on top, making swirls with a knife. Bake for 35–40 minutes, or until the top is springy to the touch.

Oven temperature
350°F/180°C

Baking time
30–35 minutes

Baking pan
8in (20cm) square cake pan, lined

Makes
16 squares

Storage
Keep for 3–4 days in the refrigerator

Freezing
1–2 months, un-iced

Marbled Brownie

Blonde Brownies

These are a less rich version of the classic brownie, with a caramel flavor. Like all brownies, they firm up as they cool, so be careful not to overbake them. Cooling them in the pan helps keep them moist.

INGREDIENTS

⅓ cup (75g) granulated sugar
2 tbsp water
12 tbsp (180g) unsalted butter
1 cup (180g) light brown sugar
2 eggs, lightly beaten
1½ cups (200g) self-rising flour, sifted
⅛ tsp salt
¾ cup (90g) walnuts, chopped
3oz (90g) semisweet chocolate, chopped into pea-size pieces (see page 32)

1 Heat the granulated sugar gently in a small, heavy-based saucepan until the sugar melts and caramelizes. Swirl the pan when the sugar colors and take it off the heat when it becomes a dark caramel color. Add the water to the caramel at arm's length to avoid splashes.

2 Cream the butter, then beat in the brown sugar until the mixture is light and fluffy. Gradually add the eggs to the creamed ingredients. Stir in the caramel, heating gently to thin it if it has become too thick to pour readily.

3 Sift the flour and salt together and fold into the mixture. Fold in the walnuts and chocolate.

4 Turn the mixture into the prepared pan. Bake in the preheated oven for 40–45 minutes, or until a skewer inserted into the center comes out clean. Run a knife around the inside of the pan and let the cake cool for 10 minutes. Turn out and cut into squares.

Oven temperature
350°F/180°C

Baking time
40–45 minutes

Baking pan
8in (20cm) square cake pan, lined

Makes
16 squares

Storage
Keep for 3–4 days in an airtight container

Freezing
2 months

Chocolate Muffins

A light-textured chocolate muffin with a surprise hidden inside. Delicious served with vanilla ice cream.

INGREDIENTS

½ cup (125g) unsalted butter

⅓ cup (90g) granulated sugar

2 tbsp dark brown sugar

2 eggs

1 tsp vanilla extract

1½ cups (200g) self-rising cake flour or self-rising flour

2 tbsp cocoa powder

¼ tsp salt

⅔ cup (150ml) milk

2oz (60g) semisweet chocolate, cut into ½in (1cm) pieces

1 Cream the butter, beat in both sugars, and mix until the consistency is light and fluffy. Lightly mix the eggs and vanilla and gradually beat them into the creamed ingredients.

2 Sift the flour, cocoa, and salt together twice. Fold the dry ingredients into the butter mixture, alternating with the milk.

3 Half-fill the paper cups in the muffin pan with the mixture. Put a few pieces of chocolate on top and cover with a spoonful of the mixture. Half-fill any empty wells in the pan with water to help ensure even baking.

4 Bake in the preheated oven for about 20 minutes, or until the muffins have risen and are springy to the touch. Remove from the muffin pan and cool on a wire rack. The muffins are at their best when freshly baked.

Oven temperature
375°F/190°C

Baking time
20 minutes

Baking pan
Muffin pan with 1in (2.5cm)-deep wells, lined with paper baking cups

Makes
12 muffins

Storage
Keep for 3–4 days in an airtight container, but best eaten as soon as made

Fudge Fingers

These fudge bars can be stirred up in a minute and make a rich treat to serve with coffee or as a pick-up snack.

INGREDIENTS

½ cup (75g) hazelnuts, toasted and skinned (see page 38)

10oz (300g) semisweet chocolate

10 tbsp (150g) unsalted butter

¼ tsp salt

5oz (150g) graham crackers, cut into ½in (1cm) pieces

1 Roughly chop the toasted and skinned hazelnuts.

2 Carefully melt the chocolate, butter, and salt together over very low heat or in the top of a double boiler (see page 32). Mix the graham crackers and the nuts into the chocolate.

3 Turn the mixture into the prepared pan and press it into a smooth layer. Chill for at least 2 hours before cutting into fingers.

VARIATION
Replace the hazelnuts with a mixture of walnuts or almonds and raisins, chopped citrus peel, or crystallized ginger.

Baking pan
7in (18cm) square pan, lined.

Makes
14 fingers

Storage
Keep for 1 week, tightly wrapped, in the refrigerator

Bishop's Bread

Chocolate, lemon, and nuts enhance the flavor of this moist, buttery tea bread.

INGREDIENTS

¾ cup (100g) self-rising flour
2 tbsp cornstarch
¼ tsp baking powder
9 tbsp (140g) lightly salted butter
½ cup (140g) superfine sugar
2 eggs
1 tsp vanilla extract
2 tbsp golden raisins
¼ cup (30g) walnuts, chopped
zest of ½ lemon, grated
1½ oz (40g) semisweet chocolate, chopped into pea-size pieces (see page 32)
confectioners' sugar, to decorate

1 Sift the flour, cornstarch, and baking powder together three times.

2 Cream the butter and sugar together until light and fluffy. Lightly mix the eggs and vanilla extract together and gradually beat them into the creamed ingredients.

3 Carefully fold the dry ingredients into the mixture, a third at a time, using a large metal spoon. Be careful not to overmix. Fold in the raisins, walnuts, lemon zest, and chocolate.

4 Pour the mixture into the prepared pan and bake in the center of the preheated oven for 45–50 minutes, or until a skewer inserted in the center comes out clean.

5 Cool the cake in the pan for 5 minutes before turning out onto a wire rack to finish cooling. Dust the cake with confectioners' sugar before serving.

Oven temperature
350°F/180°C

Baking time
45–50 minutes

Baking pan
1lb (500g) loaf pan, greased and lined

Makes
10 slices

Storage
Keeps for 4–5 days in an airtight container

Freezing
1–2 months

Chocolate-Dipped Meringues

Meringues are versatile and easy to make – both basic white meringues and the chocolate-flavored variation I have included here. They can be served with ice cream or summer berries, or filled with different-flavored creams.

INGREDIENTS

4 egg whites
pinch of cream of tartar
¾ cup (200g) superfine sugar
5oz (150g) semisweet chocolate, melted (see page 33)
1 cup (250ml) heavy cream

1 Whisk the egg whites with the cream of tartar until they form soft peaks. Whisk in the sugar, a few tablespoons at a time, until the meringue mixture is very stiff.

2 Take up spoonfuls of the mixture and use a second spoon to push them in oval shapes onto the prepared baking sheets, leaving ¾in (2cm) spaces between each to allow for spreading. You should get about 36 meringues.

3 Bake in the preheated oven for 1 hour. Turn off the oven and leave the meringues inside until cool. Carefully peel them off the parchment.

4 Melt the chocolate (see page 33). Dip the bottom of each meringue shell in chocolate and put them, dipped side down, on baking parchment to set.

5 Whip the cream until it forms soft peaks. Sandwich the meringues together in pairs with the cream and place them on their sides in paper baking cups.

VARIATION
Chocolate Meringues
Sift 2½ tablespoons cocoa powder over the meringue mixture and fold it in, with ½ teaspoon vanilla extract. Spoon the mixture onto prepared baking sheets and bake as for the basic meringues. The mixture could also be piped from a nylon pastry bag fitted with a medium nozzle.

Oven temperature
250°F/120°C

Baking time
1 hour

Baking pans
Two flat baking sheets, lined with baking parchment

Makes
18 double meringues

Storage
Undipped and unfilled meringues keep for 1–2 months in an airtight container

Profiteroles

Profiteroles are always a welcome treat. Fill them with ice cream or a flavored whipped cream, like the coffee cream I suggest here.

INGREDIENTS

For the choux pastry

1 cup (100g) unbleached all-purpose flour

5 tbsp (75g) unsalted butter, cut into small pieces

¾ cup (175ml) water

½ tsp salt

2–3 eggs

For the coffee cream filling

1¼ cups (300ml) heavy cream

2 tbsp superfine sugar

2 tsp instant coffee dissolved in 2 tbsp hot water

For the chocolate sauce

⅓ cup (90ml) water

2 tbsp butter

5oz (150g) semisweet chocolate, chopped (see page 32)

2 tbsp Grand Marnier

1 Sift the flour onto a square of waxed paper.

2 Put the butter, water, and salt in a saucepan and bring to a boil. Off the heat, tip the flour all at once into the pan and beat it in at once, using a wooden spoon. Continue to beat over very low heat until the mixture is smooth and pulls away from the sides of the pan (see steps 1–2, below).

3 Take off the heat, cool slightly, and gradually beat in 2 of the eggs, mixing each addition in well before adding the next. Add only enough of the third egg to make a mixture that just falls from the spoon (see steps 3–4, below).

4 Spoon the mixture into a pastry bag fitted with a ½in (1cm) plain nozzle. Pipe small mounds of mixture 2in (5cm) apart onto the prepared baking sheet. Bake in the preheated oven for 20–25 minutes, or until crisp. Pierce the bottom of each shell with a skewer. Turn off the oven and return the profiteroles to it for 5 minutes, leaving the oven door ajar.

5 For the coffee cream filling, whip the cream with the other ingredients. Halve the profiteroles horizontally and spoon some cream into the bottom half of each shell.

6 For the chocolate sauce, bring the water and butter to a boil, take off the heat, and stir in the chocolate and liqueur. The sauce can be served hot or cold, with the profiteroles or separately in a pitcher.

Oven temperature
400°F/200°C

Baking time
20–25 minutes

Baking pan
Flat baking sheet, greased

Makes
About 48 profiteroles

Storage
Keep for 24 hours, unfilled, in an air-tight container

Freezing
2 months, unfilled; thaw, then heat in oven preheated to 350°F/180°C for a few minutes to restore crispness

How to make choux pastry

1 *Sift the flour onto a square of waxed paper. Melt the butter, water, and salt together in a heavy-based saucepan and bring to a fast, rolling boil.*

2 *Take the pan off the heat and tip in the flour. Over low heat, beat the mixture rapidly with a wooden spoon to form a smooth paste that leaves the sides of the pan cleanly .*

3 *Begin beating two of the eggs into the cooled mixture, a little at a time and beating in each addition thoroughly, until the mixture is smooth and glossy.*

Éclairs

The delectable combination of crisp light choux pastry covered in chocolate and filled with a vanilla-flavored cream ensures the continuing popularity of this classic.

INGREDIENTS

For the choux pastry

1 quantity choux pastry (see Profiteroles, opposite)

For the chocolate icing

¼ cup (30g) cocoa powder

2 tbsp superfine sugar

5 tbsp (75ml) water

1½ cups (180g) confectioners' sugar

For the crème pâtissière

2 cups (500ml) milk

1 vanilla bean, split lengthwise

6 egg yolks

½ cup (125g) granulated sugar

⅓ cup (50g) all-purpose flour, sifted

1 Make the choux pastry as for Profiteroles. Spoon into a pastry bag fitted with a ½in (1cm) plain nozzle. Pipe twelve 3in (7cm) strips of the pastry mixture, spaced well apart, onto the prepared baking sheet.

2 Bake in the preheated oven for 20–25 minutes until crisp and dry. Slice the éclairs in half lengthwise while still warm to release the steam. Put on a wire rack to cool.

3 For the chocolate glaze, put the cocoa, superfine sugar, and water in a small saucepan and bring to a boil, stirring constantly. Remove from the heat and sift in the confectioners' sugar. Stir until smoothly blended.

4 Dip the tops of the éclairs into the glaze while it is still warm. Leave on a wire rack to set, chocolate side up.

FOR CREME PATISSIERE

1 For the crème pâtissière, bring the milk and vanilla bean to a boil. Remove from the heat, cover, and leave for 15 minutes to infuse.

2 Beat the egg yolks and sugar until thick and light, then stir in the flour. Remove the bean from the milk and return the milk to a boil. (The bean can be dried and put in a jar of sugar, for vanilla sugar, if desired.)

3 Turn off the heat and whisk in the egg mixture. Return to low heat; cook, whisking, until the mixture thickens. Simmer for at least 5 minutes to ensure the flour loses its uncooked taste.

4 Put plastic wrap on the surface to prevent a skin from forming and set aside to cool. Spoon the cooled cream into the bottom half of each éclair. Replace the tops and serve as soon as possible.

Oven temperature
400°F/200°C

Baking time
20–25 minutes

Baking pan
Flat baking sheet, greased

Makes
12 éclairs

Storage
Best eaten as soon as made

Pile profiteroles in a pyramid and serve them with a chocolate sauce

4 Beat in only enough of the third egg, which will probably just be half of it, to make a mixture that falls reluctantly off the spoon. Any leftover egg could be used for glazing.

Piping choux pastry onto a baking sheet

Cookies

Among these hard-to-resist cookies are the elegant Florentine, a luxury version of the brandy snap, and the North American favorite, Toll House Cookie. There is also a chocolate version of Italy's popular biscotti, which is perfect for dunking in coffee or dessert wine. Cookies can be time-consuming to make, but planning ahead and having all ingredients at room temperature greatly cuts the time needed. They keep well, too, so it can save time to bake a double batch or two of different cookies in one session.

Florentines

Despite their delicate appearance, these special cookies are not at all difficult to make. They can be coated in white or milk chocolate as well as the more traditional semisweet chocolate. Lines of leftover melted chocolate can be drizzled over for an eye-catching extra decoration.

INGREDIENTS

For the cookies

3 tbsp lightly salted butter
5 tbsp heavy cream
¼ cup (60g) superfine sugar
¼ cup (30g) hazelnuts
2 tbsp slivered almonds
¼ cup (45g) mixed peel and chopped glacé cherries, mixed
¼ cup (30g) all-purpose flour
pinch of salt

For the topping

2oz (60g) white chocolate
2oz (60g) semisweet chocolate

1 Melt the butter, cream, and sugar together in a saucepan and slowly bring to boiling point. Remove the pan from the heat and add the hazelnuts, almonds, mixed peel, and glacé cherries. When well mixed in, stir in the flour and salt.

2 Drop rounded teaspoons of the mixture 3in (7cm) apart onto the prepared baking sheets. Flatten with a wet fork.

3 Bake in the preheated oven for about 10 minutes, or until the edges are golden brown. For more perfect rounds, quickly gather the edges inside a 3in (7cm) cookie cutter. Let the cookies cool on the baking sheets for 5 minutes until firm, then carefully remove to a wire rack to cool completely.

4 Melt the chocolates for the topping separately (see page 33). Spread the undersides of the cookies with one of the chocolates and let set, chocolate side up, on a wire rack. Before the chocolate has fully set, mark wavy lines on it with a fork or confectioner's comb. Drizzle lines of leftover chocolate over the cookies.

Oven temperature
350°F/180°C

Baking time
10 minutes

Baking pans
Two flat baking sheets, greased

Makes
24 cookies

Storage
Keep for 1 week in an airtight container

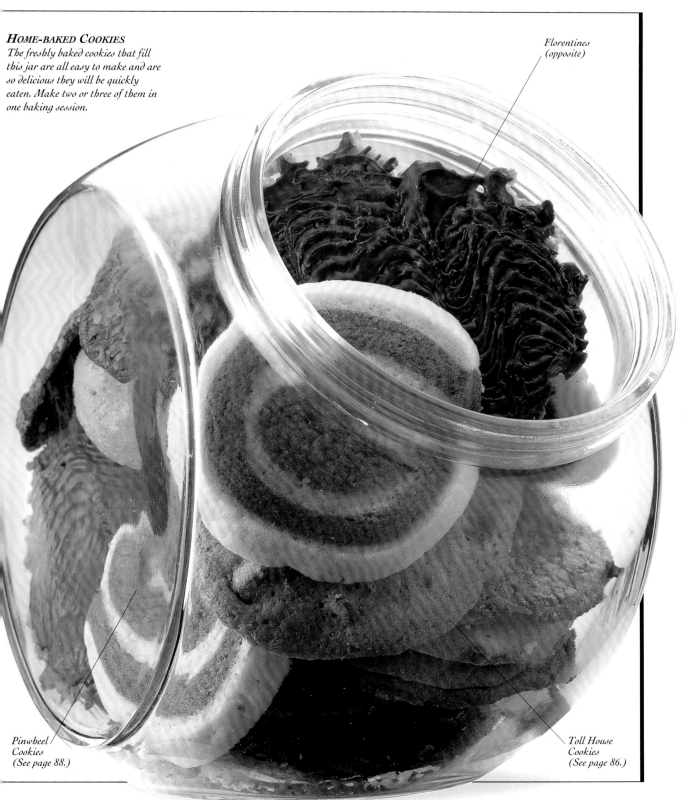

HOME-BAKED COOKIES
The freshly baked cookies that fill
this jar are all easy to make and are
so delicious they will be quickly
eaten. Make two or three of them in
one baking session.

Florentines
(opposite)

Pinwheel
Cookies
(See page 88.)

Toll House
Cookies
(See page 86.)

Toll House Cookies

These are all-time favorites and justifiably so. Almost every baker in North America has its own version of these irresistible cookies. This is one of the best; for a thinner, crisper cookie, add 2–3 tablespoons of water to the mixture.

INGREDIENTS

½ cup (125g) butter

3 tbsp vanilla granulated sugar

⅓ cup (90g) dark brown sugar

1 egg

1 tsp vanilla extract

1 cup (125g) all-purpose flour

½ tsp baking soda

½ tsp salt

4oz (125g) semisweet chocolate, chopped into pea-size pieces (see page 32)

½ cup (60g) walnuts, chopped

1 Cream the butter, beat in the two sugars, and mix until the consistency is light and fluffy. Lightly mix the egg and vanilla and gradually beat them into the creamed ingredients.

2 Sift the flour, baking soda, and salt together and fold into the mixture. Stir in the chopped chocolate and nuts.

3 Spoon heaped teaspoons of the mixture onto the prepared baking sheets, spaced well apart to give the cookies room to spread.

4 Bake the cookies in batches in the preheated oven for 10–12 minutes, until lightly browned. Transfer to a wire rack to cool.

Oven temperature
350°F/180°C

Baking time
10–12 minutes per batch

Baking pans
Two or three flat baking sheets, greased

Makes
About 30 cookies

Storage
Keep for 1 week in an airtight container

White Chocolate Chip Cookies

A variation of the Toll House Cookies, these butterscotch-flavored crisp cookies are enriched with nuggets of white chocolate.

INGREDIENTS

½ cup (125g) unsalted butter

¼ cup (60g) light brown sugar

⅓ cup (75g) dark brown sugar

1 egg

1 tsp vanilla extract

1½ cups (180g) all-purpose flour

½ tsp baking soda

½ tsp salt

5oz (150g) white chocolate, chopped into pea-size pieces (see page 32)

½ cup (60g) pecans, chopped

1 Cream the butter, beat in the two sugars, and mix until the mixture is light and fluffy. Lightly mix the egg and vanilla and gradually beat them into the creamed ingredients.

2 Sift the flour with the baking soda and salt and fold into the mixture. Stir in the chocolate and nuts.

3 Form the dough into 1½in (3.5cm) balls and put on the prepared baking sheets, 1in (2.5cm) apart. Flatten them with the palm of your hand.

4 Bake in the preheated oven for 10–12 minutes. Cool on the baking sheets for a few minutes, then remove to a wire rack to cool completely.

Oven temperature
350°F/180°C

Baking time
10–12 minutes

Baking pans
Two flat baking sheets, lined with baking parchment

Makes
18 cookies

Storage
Keep for 1 week in an airtight container

Chocolate Chip Peanut Butter Cookies

Children enjoy these cookies. The addition of peanut butter gives them a crumbly texture and lots of flavor.

INGREDIENTS

½ cup (125g) unsalted butter

½ cup (90g) dark brown sugar

6 tbsp (125g) chunky peanut butter

1 egg

1 tsp vanilla extract

1½ cups (180g) all-purpose flour

½ tsp baking soda

½ tsp salt

4oz (125g) semisweet chocolate, chopped into pea-size pieces (see page 32)

1 Cream the butter and sugar together until the mixture is light and fluffy. Blend in the peanut butter. Lightly mix the egg and vanilla together and gradually beat into the creamed ingredients.

2 Sift the flour with the baking soda and salt and fold into the mixture. Stir in the chopped chocolate.

3 Put heaped teaspoons of the mixture 1½in (3.5cm) apart on the prepared baking sheets and flatten them with a wet spoon. Bake in the preheated oven for 10–12 minutes. Cool on a wire rack.

Oven temperature
375°F/190°C

Baking time
10–12 minutes

Baking pans
Two flat baking sheets, greased

Makes
18 cookies

Storage
Keep for 1 week in an airtight container

Mocha Cookies

A very rich, irresistible cookie that is crisp on the outside with a meltingly moist interior.

INGREDIENTS

11oz (325g) semisweet chocolate, coarsely chopped (see page 32)

½ cup (125g) unsalted butter

¾ cup (90g) all-purpose flour

½ tsp baking powder

½ tsp salt

4 eggs

1 cup (225g) superfine sugar

1 tbsp instant espresso coffee powder

2 tsp vanilla extract

1½ cups (200g) semisweet chocolate chips

1 Melt the chocolate and butter together over low heat (see page 34). Set aside to cool.

2 Sift the flour, baking powder, and salt together.

3 Beat the eggs and sugar until pale and thick. Add the coffee powder and vanilla extract. Stir in the melted chocolate. Fold in the flour mixture, then add the chocolate chips. Leave the mixture in a cool place for 15 minutes.

4 Put level tablespoons of the dough on the prepared baking sheets 2in (5cm) apart to allow the cookies to spread.

5 Bake the cookies in batches in the preheated oven for 10–12 minutes, or until they are shiny and cracked on top. Leave the cookies on the baking sheets until cool, then remove to a wire rack.

Oven temperature
350°F/180°C

Baking time
10–12 minutes per batch

Baking pans
Two or three flat baking sheets, lined with baking parchment

Makes
32 cookies

Storage
Keep for 1–2 weeks in an airtight container

Chocolate Shortbread

These shortbreads have a melt-in-the-mouth lightness. They make an elegant accompaniment to fruit salad or ice cream.

INGREDIENTS

For the cookies

⅓ cup (90g) superfine sugar

1¼ cups (225g) all-purpose flour, sifted

pinch of salt

⅓ cup (45g) cocoa powder, sifted

1 cup (250g) unsalted butter, cut into pea-size pieces

For the decoration

4oz (125g) semisweet chocolate

1oz (30g) white chocolate

1 For the cookies, mix the sugar, flour, salt, and cocoa powder in a bowl. Add the butter and rub in with the fingertips to form a dough.

2 Put the dough on a lightly floured surface and roll it out to ¼in (5mm) thick. Cut out cookies with a 2in (5cm) heart-shaped cutter (or other shape, if desired). Put the cookies on the prepared baking sheets, making sure that they do not touch one another, and chill for 1 hour.

3 Bake in the preheated oven for about 45 minutes, or until firm. Cool on the baking sheets for a few minutes before removing them to a wire rack to cool completely.

4 For the decoration, melt the chocolates separately. Put the melted white chocolate into a paper piping bag, snipping a very tiny hole in the point.

5 Spread semisweet chocolate over the cookies. Before it has set, pipe the white chocolate over the cookies, in lines for a feathered pattern, or swirls for a marbled pattern (see page 47). Let the chocolate set.

Oven temperature
250°F/120°C

Baking time
45 minutes

Baking pans
Two flat baking sheets, lined with baking parchment

Makes
36 small shortbreads

Storage
Keep for 1 week, un-iced, in an airtight container

Pinwheel Cookies

The dough for these cookies, and the variation I suggest, will keep for 2 weeks in the refrigerator ready to be sliced and baked into fresh cookies at a moment's notice.

INGREDIENTS

3 cups (375g) all-purpose flour

14 tbsp (200g) lightly salted butter

1 cup (250g) superfine sugar

2 eggs

pinch of salt

1 tsp vanilla extract

1oz (30g) semisweet chocolate, melted (see page 33)

1 Sift the flour and set aside.

2 Cream the butter, then beat in the sugar until light and fluffy. Lightly beat the eggs with the salt and vanilla extract and gradually add to the creamed mixture. Stir in the sifted flour.

3 Divide the dough in half. Knead the melted chocolate into half the dough. Wrap the doughs separately and chill for 30 minutes.

4 Roll the doughs, between sheets of plastic wrap, into oblongs about 3in (7cm) wide and ¼in (5mm) thick. Put the dark dough on top of the light dough and roll up like a jelly roll. Wrap tightly and chill for 4 hours, or freeze for 1 hour.

5 Cut the firm roll of dough into ⅜in (6mm) slices. Put them on the prepared baking sheets and bake in batches in the preheated oven for 8–10 minutes. While still hot, remove them to a flat surface or wire rack to cool.

VARIATION
Butterscotch Cookies
Substitute 1½ cups (250g) soft dark brown sugar for the superfine sugar; omit the chocolate. Leave the dough in one piece. Roll out into an oblong 3in (7cm) wide, ½in (1cm) thick. Roll up the dough and make the cookies as in steps 4 and 5.

Oven temperature
375°F/190°C

Baking time
8–10 minutes per batch

Baking pans
Two or three flat baking sheets, greased

Makes
36 cookies

Storage
Keep for 2 weeks in an airtight container

Chocolate Hazelnut Tuiles

These thin tuiles can be shaped into containers to hold fruits or ice cream. Make them even more chocolate-flavored by piping patterns of melted chocolate on them.

INGREDIENTS

¼ cup (90g) hazelnuts, toasted (see page 38)

⅓ cup (100g) superfine sugar

4 tbsp lightly salted butter

5 tsp cocoa powder

3 tbsp heavy cream

2 tbsp rum

2 large egg whites

⅓ cup (45g) all-purpose flour

1oz (30g) semisweet chocolate, to decorate

1 Chop a third of the hazelnuts and set aside. Finely grind the remaining nuts and the sugar together.

2 Cream the butter, then stir in the nut/sugar mixture, cocoa, cream, and rum. Add the egg whites, stirring only enough to blend. Sift the flour over the mixture and fold in.

3 Mark four or five circles, 4½in (11cm) in diameter, 2in (5cm) apart, on the baking sheets. Put a scant tablespoon of the mixture in the center of each circle and thinly spread it out with the back of the spoon. Sprinkle on a few pieces of the reserved chopped nuts.

4 Bake each batch separately in the preheated oven for about 5 minutes, or until the edges of the tuiles are just beginning to darken.

5 Remove the tuiles with a narrow spatula and, working quickly, put them over a rolling pin (or in a cup, if you want tuile baskets, or around a metal or paper horn). Set the baking sheet in the open oven to keep the tuiles warm and pliable.

6 Melt the semisweet chocolate (see page 33) and spoon into a paper piping bag (see page 46). Pipe patterns of chocolate on the cold and crisp tuiles.

Oven temperature
425°F/220°C

Baking time
5 minutes per batch

Baking pans
Two flat baking sheets, greased with butter and floured

Makes
16 tuiles

Storage
Keep for 1 week in an airtight container

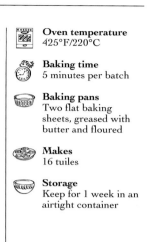

Coconut Macaroons

A chewy coconut chocolate treat. Here, I have half-dipped the macaroons in semisweet or white chocolate, then piped lines of the contrasting color over them. You could also simply dip the bottoms in melted chocolate, as for the Chocolate-Dipped Meringues (see page 81).

INGREDIENTS

4oz (125g) bittersweet chocolate
2 egg whites
pinch of salt
½ cup (100g) granulated sugar
3 cups (180g) dried coconut
1 tsp vanilla extract
2oz (60g) each semisweet and white chocolate, to decorate

1 Melt the chocolate (see page 33) and set aside to cool.

2 Whisk the egg whites with the salt until they form soft peaks. Add 3–4 tablespoons of the sugar and whisk until the mixture is glossy and firm. Fold in the remaining sugar, then the chocolate, followed by the coconut and vanilla extract.

3 Place rounded spoonfuls of the mixture 1in (2.5cm) apart on the prepared baking sheets. Bake in the preheated oven for 15–18 minutes, until the macaroons are dry on the outside but soft in the center.

4 Melt the chocolates for the decoration separately (see page 33). Half-dip the cookies into one or the other chocolate. Lay on baking parchment to set.

5 Spoon the remaining chocolate into paper piping bags and pipe contrasting lines over the macaroons.

Oven temperature
300°F/150°C

Baking time
15–18 minutes

Baking pans
Two flat baking sheets, lined with baking parchment

Makes
24 macaroons

Storage
Keep for 4–5 days in an airtight container

Chocolate Macaroons

These delicate macaroons are crisp on the outside with a soft interior. They can be sandwiched together with raspberry jam or Chocolate Ganache (see page 136).

INGREDIENTS

2 cups (225g) confectioners' sugar
¼ cup (30g) cocoa powder
1 cup (125g) ground almonds
4 egg whites
2 tbsp superfine sugar

1 Sift the confectioners' sugar and cocoa powder together. Sift the ground almonds over the top. Whisk the egg whites to soft peaks, then add the superfine sugar. Whisk until stiff. Gently fold in the confectioners' sugar mixture with a large metal spoon.

2 Fill a pastry bag, fitted with a ½in (1cm) nozzle, with the mixture. Pipe small rounds about 1in (2.5cm) in diameter, spaced 1in (2.5cm) apart, onto the prepared baking sheets. Leave at room temperature for 15 minutes.

3 Bake in the preheated oven for 10–12 minutes. Leave the oven door slightly ajar to allow steam to escape. Remove the macaroons from the oven and leave for a few minutes before lifting them off the paper.

Oven temperature
350°F/180°C

Baking time
10–12 minutes

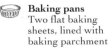
Baking pans
Two flat baking sheets, lined with baking parchment

Makes
36 macaroons

Storage
Keep for 3–4 days in an airtight container

Chocolate Walnut Cookies

These wafer-thin buttery cookies are a family favorite. They are also good made with other nuts such as hazelnuts or pecans.

INGREDIENTS
1¼ cups (200g) all-purpose flour

⅛ tsp salt

¼ cup (30g) cocoa powder

½ tsp baking soda

10 tbsp (150g) unsalted butter

1 cup (150g) dark brown sugar

2 tbsp granulated sugar

1 egg yolk

1 tsp vanilla extract

¾ cup (90g) walnuts, very finely chopped

1 Sift the flour, salt, cocoa powder, and soda together.

2 Beat the butter until soft, add both sugars, and continue to beat until well blended. Stir in the egg yolk and vanilla. Fold in the flour mixture and the walnuts. With lightly floured hands, roll the dough into a sausage shape 2in (5cm) in diameter.

3 Wrap the dough in plastic wrap and chill for at least 2 hours or freeze until the dough is very firm, about 1 hour.

4 Using a very thin, sharp knife, cut the dough into ⅛in (2.5mm) slices. Put them on the prepared baking sheets and bake in batches in the preheated oven for 8–10 minutes. Be careful not to let them burn or overcook.

5 Lift them off the paper and place on a flat surface to cool and crisp.

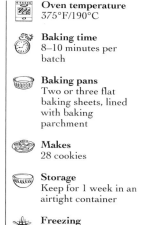

Oven temperature
375°F/190°C

Baking time
8–10 minutes per batch

Baking pans
Two or three flat baking sheets, lined with baking parchment

Makes
28 cookies

Storage
Keep for 1 week in an airtight container

Freezing
Dough freezes for 1–2 months

Chocolate Almond Biscotti

In northern Italy these firm, dry cookies are served accompanied by a glass of Vin Santo. The biscotti are dipped into the sweet wine to soften and to soak up the wine's rich taste.

INGREDIENTS
¾ cup (125g) almonds

2½ cups (300g) all-purpose flour

1 tsp baking powder

½ tsp salt

¾ cup (180g) superfine sugar

zest of ½ orange, very finely chopped

2 eggs

2 egg yolks

3oz (90g) semisweet chocolate, chopped into pea-size pieces (see page 32)

1 egg white, lightly beaten

1 Toast the almonds lightly on an ungreased baking sheet in the preheated oven for about 10 minutes. When they have cooled, chop half of them coarsely and set aside.

2 Finely grind the remaining almonds in a processor or blender. Sift the flour, baking powder, and salt into a bowl. Stir in the sugar, ground nuts, and orange zest. Make a well in the center of the dry ingredients and add the whole eggs and yolks. Stir from the center, incorporating the flour, little by little, until the mixture starts to stick together. Add the chopped nuts and the chocolate pieces.

3 Turn out onto a floured surface and, handling the dough as lightly as possible, divide it into four equal parts. Form each into a sausage shape about 9 x 1½in (23 x 4cm) and brush with the egg white. Place them, spaced apart, on the greased baking sheet. Bake in the preheated oven for 20 minutes. Remove from the oven. Reduce the oven temperature to the lower setting.

4 Cut the dough into ½in (1cm) slices on the diagonal. Lay the slices on the ungreased baking sheets.

5 Bake, turning once, for 25–30 minutes. Remove from the oven and leave on the baking sheet to cool completely.

Oven temperature
375°F/190°C; then 275°F/140°C

Baking time
20 minutes first baking; 25–30 minutes second baking

Baking pans
Flat baking sheet, greased and floured; one or two flat baking sheets, ungreased

Makes
40 cookies

Storage
Keep for 2–3 weeks in an airtight container

Pies & Tarts

Fill a crisp pastry shell or crunchy cookie crust with sumptuous chocolate to create a perfect dessert combination. There are so many delectable choices, from Chocolate Pear Tart, in which the fruit enhances the taste of the chocolate, to light-as-air Chocolate Chiffon Pie topped with swirls of whipped cream, and a chocolate-rich version of Banoffee Pie. Ice cream and whipped cream, the classic accompaniments for dessert pies, are particularly apt when served with chocolate, for they intensify its unique flavor.

Mississippi Mud Pie

A favorite recipe in the American South, this pie has a luscious chocolate filling, with a dash of coffee flavoring, enclosed in a light egg pastry shell.

INGREDIENTS

For the pastry shell

1 quantity Chocolate Pecan Pie pastry (see page 96)

For the filling

10 tbsp (150g) butter

1oz (30g) semisweet chocolate, chopped (see page 32)

6 tbsp (45g) cocoa powder, sifted

2 tsp instant espresso coffee powder

3 eggs

1 cup (250g) superfine sugar

2 tbsp sour cream

3 tbsp corn syrup

1 tsp vanilla extract

white, milk, and semisweet chocolate curls, to decorate (see page 43)

1 Allow the pastry to come to room temperature. Knead it briefly, then roll it out on a lightly floured surface. Use the pastry to line the prepared pan, rolling it out a little thinner than for the Chocolate Pecan Pie. Chill the pastry shell while preparing the filling.

2 Put a baking sheet in the lower third of the oven and preheat the oven.

3 For the filling, gently melt the butter in a small saucepan. Remove from the heat and stir in the chocolate, cocoa powder, and coffee, stirring until the chocolate has melted. Set aside.

4 Beat the eggs and sugar together until the mixture is creamy and blended, then add the sour cream, corn syrup, and vanilla extract. Stir in the chocolate and butter mixture.

5 Pour the filling into the pastry shell. Bake on the hot baking sheet in the preheated oven for 35–40 minutes, or until the filling puffs up and forms a crust. Remove the pie to a wire rack to cool. The filling will sink a little and may crack slightly as it cools.

6 Before serving, decorate the pie with chocolate curls: a mixture of different colored curls looks impressive. Vanilla ice cream is an excellent accompaniment for this pie.

 Oven temperature 350°F/180°C

Baking time 35–40 minutes

Baking pan 1½in (3.5cm)-deep, 9in (23cm)-diameter, loose-based tart pan, greased

Makes 8–10 slices

Storage Keeps for 2 days in the refrigerator

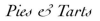

MISSISSIPPI MUD PIE

This richly dark pie has a wonderfully smooth filling, containing two kinds of chocolate baked in a sweet pastry shell. Elegant chocolate curls complete a memorable dessert pie.

Large chocolate curls make a stylish topping

The sweet, creamy filling gives this pie its name

Chocolate Mousse Pie

This pie's shell is given texture and flavor by the addition of finely ground hazelnuts. The baked filling, based on eggs, cream, and chocolate, has a luxury touch of brandy or rum, added just before baking.

DECORATING THE PIE
The top of the Chocolate Mousse Pie cracks as it cools. Large chocolate curls and a dusting of cocoa powder help to cover the cracks and also integrate them into an eye-appealing decoration.

INGREDIENTS

For the pastry shell

½ cup (60g) toasted and skinned hazelnuts (see page 38), finely ground

1½ cups (165g) all-purpose flour, sifted

2 tbsp superfine sugar

½ cup (125g) lightly salted butter, diced

1 small egg, lightly beaten

a little ice water

For the filling

4oz (125g) semisweet chocolate

4 tbsp butter

2 eggs

½ cup (100g) superfine sugar

2 tbsp flour

4 tbsp heavy cream

1½ tbsp rum or brandy

For the decoration

semisweet chocolate curls (see page 43)

cocoa powder

1 For the pastry, put the ground hazelnuts, flour, and sugar in a large bowl. Add the butter and rub in with the fingertips until the mixture resembles fine bread crumbs. Mix in sufficient egg and, if necessary, water, to make a stiff dough (the mixture should stick together in small clumps).

2 Turn out the dough onto a lightly floured surface and form into a ball. Wrap in plastic wrap and chill for 30 minutes.

3 Preheat the oven to the higher temperature, putting a baking sheet in the lower third of the oven. Roll out the dough

on a lightly floured surface and use to line the tart pan. Prick the bottom with a fork. Line the pastry with waxed paper weighed down with dried beans (to bake the shell "blind").

4 Put the pan on the hot baking sheet and bake for 10 minutes. Remove the paper and beans and bake for another 5–8 minutes. Cool on a wire rack. Reduce the oven temperature to the lower setting.

5 For the filling, melt the chocolate and butter together (see page 34). Set aside to cool. Whisk the eggs and sugar in a large heatproof bowl set over hot water for about 10 minutes, or until the mixture forms a ribbon when the whisk is lifted. Sift the flour over the top and fold it in. Fold in the chocolate, cream, and alcohol.

6 Pour the filling into the pastry shell and bake on the hot baking sheet for 15 minutes. Remove to a wire rack to cool.

7 To decorate, arrange the chocolate curls on top of the pie and sift a dusting of cocoa over them.

Oven temperature
400°F/200°C;
then
375°F/190°C

Baking time
15–18 minutes for the pastry shell; 15 minutes for the pie

Baking pan
1½in (3.5cm)-deep, 9in (23cm)-diameter, loose-based tart pan, greased

Makes
8 slices

Storage
Keeps for 2 days in the refrigerator, but best eaten as soon as made

Chocolate Chiffon Pie

Stiffly beaten egg whites give an airy lightness to the deliciously creamy, richly flavored chocolate custard for this pie's filling.

INGREDIENTS

For the crust

2 cups (150g) graham crackers, crushed

1 cup (100g) ground hazelnuts, walnuts, or almonds

6 tbsp (90g) unsalted butter, melted

For the filling

2 tsp gelatin

2 tbsp cold water

2 eggs, separated

1 cup (150g) superfine sugar

1 cup (250ml) milk

7oz (200g) semisweet chocolate, chopped into small pieces (see page 32)

2 tsp vanilla extract

1¼ cups (300ml) heavy cream

pinch of salt

For the decoration

⅔ cup (150ml) heavy cream, whipped

semisweet chocolate curls (see page 43)

1 Put the cracker crumbs and nuts in a bowl, pour in the butter, and mix together lightly with a fork. Turn into the tart pan, pressing the mixture in an even layer over the sides and bottom to make a crust.

2 Bake the crust in the preheated oven for 10 minutes. Cool on a wire rack. Chill in the pan until needed.

3 For the filling, put the gelatin and water in a cup and leave until the gelatin is spongy, about 5 minutes. Set the cup in hot water until the gelatin has dissolved.

4 Whisk the egg yolks with ⅓ cup (90g) of the sugar. Bring the milk to a boil, pour it over the egg yolks, whisking constantly, then return the mixture to the saucepan. Stir with a wooden spoon over low heat until the mixture thickens enough to coat the spoon. Do not allow it to boil, or it will curdle. Remove the custard from the heat and stir in the gelatin. Add the chocolate pieces and vanilla and stir until blended. Set aside to cool.

5 Lightly whip the cream. Fold it into the cooled chocolate mixture with a large metal spoon. Whisk the egg whites with the salt until stiff, add the remaining sugar, and whisk until the egg whites form stiff peaks. Carefully fold the egg whites into the mixture, making sure that the chiffon is thoroughly blended without overmixing. Pour into the crust, smoothing the top with a narrow spatula. Chill the pie for at least 2 hours or until set, keeping it in the refrigerator until needed.

Oven temperature
350°F/180°C

Baking time
10 minutes

Baking pan
1½in (3.5cm)-deep, 9in (23cm)-diameter, loose-based tart pan

Makes
8 slices

Storage
Keeps for 2 days in the refrigerator

* Warning
This recipe contains uncooked egg whites (see page 9)

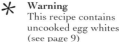

DECORATING THE PIE
Rosettes of firmly whipped cream (see page 48) are piped around the top edge of the Chocolate Chiffon Pie. Small chocolate curls, set on top of the cream rosettes, provide a final neat touch of chocolate.

Chocolate Pecan Pie

This is a variation of the North American favorite, Pecan Pie. The dark chocolate filling is rum-flavored.

INGREDIENTS

For the pastry shell

1½ cups (190g) all-purpose flour
2 tbsp superfine sugar
½ tsp salt
7 tbsp (100g) chilled unsalted butter, cut into small pieces
1 egg yolk
2 tbsp ice water

For the filling

4 tbsp butter
2 tbsp cocoa powder
1 cup (250ml) corn syrup
3 eggs
½ cup (90g) dark brown sugar
2 tbsp rum
2 cups (250g) pecans

1 To make the pastry, sift the flour, sugar, and salt into a bowl. Rub the butter into the flour with your fingertips until the mixture resembles oatmeal. Blend the egg yolk with the water and fork it lightly into the mixture until it sticks together in small clumps.

2 Form the dough into a ball, wrap in plastic wrap and chill for 30 minutes. Roll out the pastry and line the tart pan. Chill while making the filling.

3 Put a baking sheet in the oven while it is preheating. For the filling, gently melt the butter, then, off the heat, stir in the cocoa and corn syrup. Lightly beat the eggs with the sugar and rum. Stir in the syrup mixture. Chop half the nuts and add to the mixture. Pour into the pastry shell. Arrange the remaining nuts over the top.

4 Bake the pie on the hot baking sheet in the preheated oven for 35–40 minutes, or until the filling is just set. Cover the pie with foil if the pastry becomes too dark. Serve the pie warm or at room temperature.

 **Oven temperature**
350°F/180°C

 Baking time
35–40 minutes

Baking pan
9½ in (24cm) loose-based tart pan, greased

Makes
8–10 slices

Storage
Keeps for 2 days in an airtight container in the refrigerator

Chocolate Fruit Tartlets

These delicious tartlets are filled with cream and fresh fruits. The chocolate pastry base is easy to make; the ingredients are mixed in a saucepan.

INGREDIENTS

For the pastry

10 tbsp (150g) lightly salted butter, cut into small pieces
¼ cup (60g) dark brown sugar
3 tbsp cocoa powder
2 cups (250g) all-purpose flour
1 small egg white

For the filling and decoration

½ cup (150g) fruit jelly
1 tbsp water
⅔ cup (150ml) heavy cream, lightly whipped
1½lb (750g) fresh berries
chocolate leaves (see page 43)

1 For the pastry, stir the butter, sugar, and cocoa together in a saucepan over low heat until the butter has melted and the ingredients are blended. Take the saucepan off the heat and stir in the flour, then enough egg white to make a firm dough. Wrap in plastic wrap and chill for 15 minutes.

2 Divide the chilled dough into eight balls. Roll each one out between sheets of plastic wrap. Using a 4in(10cm) plain cookie cutter, cut each piece of pastry into a round.

3 Line the tartlet pans with the rounds, prick the bottoms with a fork, and chill for 15 minutes.

4 Bake the pastry shells in the preheated oven for 20–25 minutes. Remove from the oven and cool on a wire rack. Take the cool shells from the pans.

 **Oven temperature**
350°F/180°C

 Baking time
20–25 minutes

Baking pans
Eight 2½in (6cm) tartlet pans

 **Makes**
8 tartlets

Storage
Unfilled pastry shells keep for 3 days, tightly wrapped

TO FINISH THE FRUIT TARTLETS

Make a fruit glaze by gently melting the fruit jelly with the water. Brush a thin layer of the glaze over the inside of the pastry shells. Whip the cream until it forms soft peaks and spoon it into the pastry shells. Spoon the fruits on top of the cream and brush them with some fruit glaze. Set chocolate leaves among them.

Fruit glaze gives the fruit a glistening finish

Semisweet chocolate leaves contrast well with the fruit

Chocolate Pear Tart

Pears and chocolate go together very well – which explains why there are so many desserts based on the combination. This recipe puts the two together in a delicious almond pastry shell. Choose a firm, ripe dessert pear, such as Comice or Williams.

INGREDIENTS

For the pastry shell

1½ cups (165g) all-purpose flour
2 tbsp superfine sugar
¼ cup (30g) ground almonds
½ tsp salt
½ cup (125g) chilled unsalted butter, diced
3–4 tbsp ice water

For the filling

4 or 5 ripe dessert pears, depending on size
1½ tbsp superfine sugar
6 tbsp (90g) unsalted butter
⅓ cup (45g) cocoa powder
1 egg
¾ cup (180g) granulated sugar
⅓ cup (45g) all-purpose flour
1 tsp vanilla extract
confectioners' sugar, to decorate

1 For the pastry, sift the flour, sugar, ground almonds, and salt into a bowl. Add the butter and rub it into the flour with your fingertips until the mixture resembles fine bread crumbs. Using a fork, mix in just enough water for the mixture to cling together in small clumps.

2 Turn out the dough onto a flat surface and form it into a ball. Wrap in plastic wrap and chill for at least 30 minutes.

3 Roll out the pastry on a lightly floured surface and line the prepared pan with it. Put it in the freezer while you prepare the pears.

4 Peel, quarter, and core the pears. Prick the pastry with a fork and sprinkle with the sugar. Arrange the pears on the uncooked pastry, put into the preheated oven, and bake for 15 minutes. Remove from the oven and set on a wire rack until ready to fill.

5 Meanwhile, complete the filling. Melt the butter, add the cocoa, and stir until smooth. Whisk the egg with the sugar, then add the cocoa mixture. Sift the flour over the top of the mixture and fold in. Stir in the vanilla extract. Pour the filling over the top of the pears and smooth into as even a layer as possible with a spatula.

6 Put the tart back in the oven for 15 minutes, or until the filling has set. Remove to a wire rack to cool. Before serving, decorate the top of the pie with a light sprinkling of confectioners' sugar.

Oven temperature
400°F/200°C

Baking time
15 minutes for the pastry shell and pears; 15–20 minutes for the pie

Baking pan
9in (23cm) loose-based tart pan, greased

Makes
8–10 slices

Storage
Keeps for 2 days in the refrigerator

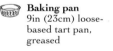

Chocolate Banoffee Pie

This dessert gets its name from its extravagant layering of ingredients: a blend of chocolate and cream in a cookie crust, then a layer of smooth toffee, topped with slices of banana, and, finally, thickly whipped cream piled high with chocolate curls.

INGREDIENTS

For the filling

2 x 14oz cans sweetened condensed milk

5oz (150g) bittersweet chocolate, melted (see page 35)

½ cup (125ml) heavy cream

1 tsp vanilla extract

For the crust

4 cups (260g) graham crackers, crushed

6 tbsp (90g) lightly salted butter, melted

For the topping

3 small ripe bananas

1¼ cups (300ml) heavy cream, whipped

semisweet, milk, and white chocolate curls (see page 43)

cocoa powder, to decorate

1 Puncture a small hole in the top of each condensed milk can. Set them in a saucepan large enough to immerse them in water. Bring to a boil and simmer for 2 hours, with the pan partially covered, adding more water as necessary. Remove the cans and cool.

2 For the crust, put the graham crackers in a bowl and pour over the butter. Mix together and turn into the prepared pan, pressing them down in an even layer, first over the sides and then on the bottom to make the crust. Bake in the preheated oven for 10 minutes. Cool the crust on a wire rack, then chill until needed.

3 Continue making the filling. Cool the chocolate to lukewarm. Whisk the cream until it is just thick and fold it into the chocolate. Fold in the vanilla. Spoon the mixture into the cooled crust, spreading it evenly. Chill until set.

4 Open the cans of cooled condensed milk, which will have cooked into a toffeelike cream. Pour into a bowl and whisk until smooth. Spoon over the chocolate layer in the crust and chill until ready to serve.

5 Finish with topping before serving. Slice the bananas and arrange them over the toffee layer. Spoon the cream on top. Pile on the chocolate curls and finish with a light dusting of cocoa powder.

Oven temperature
350°F/180°C

Baking time
10 minutes

Baking pan
1½in (3.5cm)-deep, 9in (23cm)-diameter, loose-based tart pan, greased

Makes
10–12 slices

Storage
Keeps for 2 days in the refrigerator, without banana and cream topping

Step ahead
Make toffee cream 1 day ahead, and keep in refrigerator

Hot Chocolate Desserts

What could be better to take the chill out of a cold winter's day than a hot chocolate dessert? The aroma of chocolate wafting through the air arouses the taste buds to the joy of what's to come. There are a number of delightful winter warmers to tempt the palate, from a light, airy soufflé to a sumptuous, orange-scented steamed pudding. For a special occasion, you might consider elegant, thin crepes filled with luscious chocolate cream, or an aromatic rum-flavored chocolate fondue. All warming desserts for a winter treat.

Chocolate Rum Fondue

A very satisfying dessert for chocoholics. Place the warm chocolate fondue in the center of the table with a large platter of cake, cookies, freshly prepared fruit, and forks for dipping. The fondue can be flavored with any liqueur or left plain.

Serve an eye-catching display of fruits, cakes, and cookies for dipping into the fondue

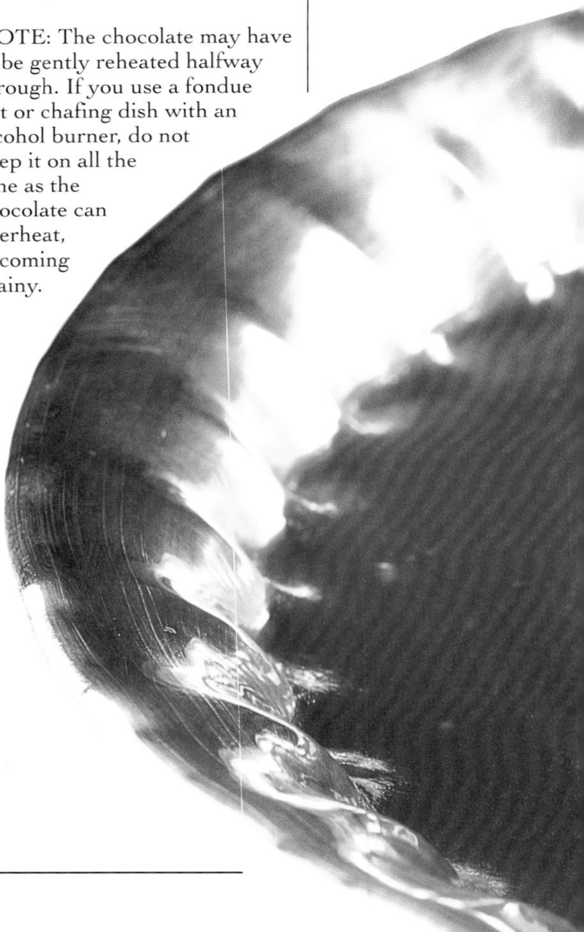

INGREDIENTS

½ cup (125g) superfine sugar

½ cup (125ml) water

6oz (180g) bittersweet chocolate

4 tbsp butter

¼ cup (50ml) rum

pound, angel food, or plain cake cut into 1in (2.5cm) cubes

ladyfingers or other plain cookies

fresh whole strawberries, small wedges of fresh pineapple or pear, orange segments, cherries, kiwifruit, and other fresh fruit

1 Put the sugar and water in a saucepan and stir over low heat until the sugar has dissolved. Remove from the heat and set aside to cool.

2 Melt the chocolate with the butter (see page 34). Stir the chocolate into the sugar syrup.

3 To serve, reheat the fondue in a microwave or in the top of a double boiler set over hot water. Stir the rum into the chocolate. Pour into a fondue pot or chafing dish. Serve the fondue warm, with fruits, cookies, and cubes of cake.

NOTE: The chocolate may have to be gently reheated halfway through. If you use a fondue pot or chafing dish with an alcohol burner, do not keep it on all the time as the chocolate can overheat, becoming grainy.

Makes
6–8 servings

Storage
Keeps for 2 days in the refrigerator

Hot Chocolate Desserts

pineapple piece

apple slice

melon ball

CHOCOLATE RUM FONDUE
Prepare bite-size pieces of fruit and cake for serving with the fondue.

plain cake

kiwifruit

Firm pieces of fresh fruit will not slip off the fondue fork

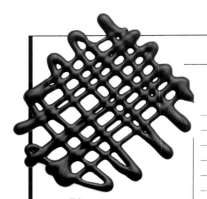

Chocolate Bread Pudding

Bread and Butter Pudding becomes much more than a nursery dish when a creamy chocolate custard is added to it.

INGREDIENTS

1 cup (250ml) heavy cream

1 cup (250ml) milk

¼ tsp salt

3 tbsp cocoa powder

3 eggs

½ cup (125g) granulated sugar

1 tsp vanilla extract

3 soft rolls

2 tbsp unsalted butter, softened

1 Bring the cream, milk, and salt slowly to a boil in a heavy-based saucepan, then remove from the heat. Sift the cocoa powder over the top and whisk until well blended. Beat the eggs and sugar together, then beat in the cocoa mixture. Add the vanilla extract.

2 Cut the rolls into thin slices and butter them. Place enough slices in the dish so that the top layer comes above the rim of the dish. Pour the custard in around the sides. The pudding can be prepared up to this stage an hour or two before baking, if desired.

3 Put the dish in a roasting pan. Fill the pan with hot water to come halfway up the sides of the dish.

4 Bake in the preheated oven for 40 minutes, or until set. If the top crusts are not crisp and brown, crisp the edges under a hot broiler. Serve the pudding with a pitcher of heavy cream, if desired.

Oven temperature
325°F/160°C

Baking time
40 minutes

Baking dish
4½ cup (1 liter) soufflé dish, greased with butter

Makes
6 servings

Step ahead
Make the pudding 1 or 2 hours before baking

Chocolate Soufflé

This is a superbly light and very chocolaty soufflé with a hint of alcohol to give it a touch of extravagance.

INGREDIENTS

3½oz (100g) semisweet chocolate

3 tbsp cornstarch

1 cup (250ml) milk

¼ cup (60g) superfine sugar

3 tbsp Grand Marnier, Cointreau, or Curaçao

2 tbsp unsalted butter

5 egg whites

pinch of salt

3 egg yolks

To serve

Crème Anglaise (see page 134) or ¾ cup (175ml) heavy cream, whipped

1 Break the chocolate into pieces and melt it (see page 33). Set aside.

2 Mix the cornstarch to a smooth paste with a few tablespoons of the milk and then gradually stir in the rest of the milk. Pour into a saucepan, add half the sugar, and bring to a boil, stirring constantly. Boil for 1 minute, remove from the heat, and stir in the chocolate

and the liqueur. Dot the surface with the butter and set aside until lukewarm.

3 Meanwhile, whisk the egg whites with the salt until they form soft peaks. Add the remaining sugar and continue whisking until the mixture is glossy and stiff.

4 Stir the egg yolks, one at a time, into the chocolate mixture, then fold in a large spoonful of the stiffly beaten whites. Carefully fold in the rest of the whites, using a large metal spoon.

5 Pour the mixture into the prepared soufflé dish and bake in the center of the preheated oven for 35 minutes, or until the soufflé has risen, the top is brown, and the center still quivers.

6 Serve the soufflé at once, with the Crème Anglaise served separately. Alternatively, serve with whipped cream.

Oven temperature
375°F/190°C

Baking time
35 minutes

Baking dish
4½ cup (1 liter) soufflé dish, buttered and lightly sprinkled with superfine sugar, and with 4in (10cm) wide baking parchment collar, also buttered and sprinkled with superfine sugar, tied around

Makes
4 servings

Chocolate Amaretti-Filled Crepes

Simple crepes become something special when given a filling full of contrasts: the taste of chocolate mingles with that of almonds; crushed cookies add crunch to the smooth mixture of chocolate and cream. You could omit flaming the pancakes with brandy, if desired.

INGREDIENTS

For the crepes

1 cup (125g) all-purpose flour
¼ tsp salt
3 eggs
1 cup (250ml) milk
2 tbsp unsalted butter, melted
oil or butter for greasing

For the filling

1 cup + 2 tbsp (275ml) milk
3 egg yolks
⅓ cup (75g) superfine sugar
¼ cup (30g) all-purpose flour
2½ oz (75g) semisweet chocolate, chopped (see page 32)
1 tbsp almond liqueur, such as Amaretto di Saronno
⅔ cup (150ml) heavy cream, lightly whipped
1 cup (60g) crushed amaretti cookies
melted butter, for brushing
sugar, for sprinkling
3–4 tbsp brandy, for flaming

1 For the crepes, sift the flour and salt into a bowl, make a well in the center, and add the eggs and milk. Whisk from the center, slowly blending the ingredients, then add the melted butter. Be careful not to overmix. Let the batter stand for at least 20 minutes. It should have the consistency of thin cream. Thin the mixture with a few tablespoons of water, if necessary.

2 Brush a 9in (23cm) crepe pan or skillet with oil. Heat the pan until very hot (a drop of batter will sizzle at once). Add a serving spoon of batter to the pan, tilting it quickly so the bottom is evenly coated. (Pour out any excess batter and adjust the amount for the next crepe.) Cook over high heat until browned, then turn the crepe over and cook for 10 seconds on the second side. It may take a few crepes before the consistency, amount of batter, and heat are just right. Stack the pancakes on a plate once they are cooked.

3 For the filling, bring the milk to a boil. Whisk the egg yolks, sugar, and flour together in a medium-size bowl. Whisk in the hot milk, then return the mixture to the saucepan and simmer for 2 minutes, stirring constantly. Remove from the heat and stir in the chocolate and liqueur. When the chocolate cream is cool, fold in the lightly whipped cream and the amaretti crumbs.

4 Grease a large flameproof gratin dish with butter. Place a spoonful of the filling on the underside of a crepe, roll it up, and place it seam side down in the dish. Alternatively, fold the crepes into quarters and overlap them in the dish. Continue until all the crepes have been used.

5 Brush the tops with melted butter and sprinkle over some sugar. Cover with a piece of baking parchment. Bake in the preheated oven for 15–20 minutes, or until hot. Heat the brandy in a small pan, flame it, and pour over the crepes. Serve immediately.

Oven temperature
350°F/180°C

Baking time
15–20 minutes

Baking dish
4½ cup (1 liter) gratin dish

Makes
About 18 crepes

Storage
Unfilled crepes keep for 2 days in the refrigerator; filling keeps for 2 days in the refrigerator

Freezing
Unfilled crepes keep for 2 months, with a layer of plastic wrap or baking parchment between each crepe

Chocolate Orange Puddings

INGREDIENTS

zest of ½ orange, finely grated

3½oz (100g) semisweet chocolate, melted (see page 33)

6 eggs, separated

¼ cup (60g) granulated sugar

1 cup (100g) ground almonds

1 cup (60g) chocolate cake crumbs

pinch of salt

For the sauce

1¼ cups (300ml) heavy cream

2–3 tbsp superfine sugar

1–2 tbsp Cointreau or other orange-flavored liqueur

These individual puddings are baked in the oven, in a bain-marie, which helps give them the texture of a light steamed pudding.

1 Mix the orange zest into the chocolate. Whisk the egg yolks with the sugar until pale. Fold in the chocolate, then the almonds and the cake crumbs.

2 Whisk the egg whites with the salt until stiff. Fold a large spoonful of the egg whites into the chocolate mixture to lighten it, then carefully fold in the remaining whites.

3 Pour the batter into the prepared molds and cover them with buttered foil. Put the molds in a roasting pan at least 2in (5cm) deep. Pour in enough hot water to come halfway up the sides of the molds.

4 Carefully put the roasting pan into the preheated oven and bake for 30 minutes, or until set.

5 To make the sauce, whip the cream until it starts to thicken slightly. Add 2 tablespoons of the sugar and 1 tablespoon of the liqueur. Taste and adjust the flavor as desired.

6 To unmold the puddings, slip a knife around the edge of the molds; put a serving plate on top of each mold, invert, and give a sharp tap to the top of the mold to help release the pudding. Spoon sauce over the puddings and serve hot.

Oven temperature
350°F/180°C

Baking time
30 minutes

Baking dishes
Eight ¾ cup (175ml) metal pudding molds, buttered and sugared

Makes
8 servings

Storage
Best eaten as soon as made

Chocolate Steamed Pudding

Cake crumbs instead of the more traditional flour produce a light and airy steamed pudding, unlike any remembered from the past. The pudding can be flavored with a favorite liqueur or with ginger, as in the variation given opposite.

INGREDIENTS

6oz (180g) chocolate cake

2 tsp ground cinnamon

3oz (90g) bittersweet chocolate

¾ cup (175ml) milk

4 tbsp butter

¼ cup (60g) granulated sugar

3 eggs, separated

1 tsp vanilla extract

small pinch of cream of tartar

To serve

Bitter Chocolate Sauce (see page 135) or ¾ cup (175ml) heavy cream, whipped

1 Break the chocolate cake into pieces. Put the pieces in a food processor or blender and pulse the machine briefly to make crumbs. Stir the cinnamon into the crumbs.

2 Melt the chocolate with the milk (see page 34), stir until smooth, and set aside.

3 Cream the butter with the sugar. Add the egg yolks, one at a time, and stir until blended. Add the chocolate milk to the cake crumbs and mix together. Turn the chocolate crumb mixture into the creamed butter and blend together. Add the vanilla.

4 Whisk the egg whites and cream of tartar until they form stiff peaks. Fold into the chocolate mixture. Turn into the buttered bowl. Cover the bowl with a pleated piece of baking parchment. Lay a dish towel over the top and tie securely under the edge of the bowl with string.

Steaming time
65–75 minutes

Baking dish
4½ cup (1 liter) pudding basin or Pyrex or metal bowl, thickly buttered

Makes
6–8 servings

Bring up the ends of the cloth and tie together to make a handle. Trim off any excess baking parchment.

5 Put a trivet or upside-down saucer in the bottom of a deep saucepan. Fill the pan with enough water to come halfway up the bowl. Heat the water and, when it is simmering, lower the pudding into the pan, cover, and steam for 65–75 minutes.

6 Carefully lift the pudding out of the water. Remove the cloth and paper. Slip a knife around the inside edge of the bowl to loosen the pudding and turn it out onto a deep serving dish.

7 Pour warm Bitter Chocolate Sauce over the pudding before serving it, with any remaining sauce served separately in a pitcher. Alternatively, serve the pudding with whipped cream.

CHOCOLATE STEAMED PUDDING

This is a deliciously rich yet light hot pudding. For a more spicy treat, try the ginger-flavored alternative below.

VARIATION
Ginger Chocolate Steamed Pudding
Omit the cinnamon and vanilla extract. Add 1 teaspoon ground ginger, 2 tablespoons chopped preserved ginger, and 1 tablespoon preserved ginger syrup.

Cold Desserts

A refreshing lightness characterizes these cool desserts, which include mousses, elegant terrines, and smooth creams. A fine array of chocolates are mixed with memorable combinations of flavorings – white chocolate with limes or semisweet chocolate with rum or an orange liqueur, for example – providing both unusual and classical partnerships. In several recipes, coffee emphasizes the richness of the chocolate. Sauces and creams, and many suggestions for elegant decorations, put the perfect finishing touch to every dessert.

Chocolate Velvet Mousse

This is a gloriously smooth mousse – hence its evocative name. It is elegant served simply with a light Crème Anglaise, but also makes an excellent base for more adventurous desserts.

INGREDIENTS

5oz (150g) bittersweet chocolate, melted

3 eggs, separated

5 tbsp (75g) unsalted butter, cut into small pieces

1 tbsp crème de cacao or Tia Maria or 2 tsp vanilla extract

1 egg white

pinch of salt

1 quantity Crème Anglaise (see page 134)

melted semisweet chocolate, to decorate (see page 33)

1 Melt the chocolate (see page 33). While still hot, beat in the egg yolks, one at a time. Stir in the butter, and when the mixture is smooth, add the liqueur or vanilla extract.

2 Whisk all 4 egg whites with a pinch of salt until the whites form stiff peaks. Fold a heaping spoonful of the whites into the chocolate mixture to lighten it, then carefully fold in the remaining whites.

3 Turn the mixture into the dish, cover, and chill until it is set – about 4 hours.

4 To serve, pour Crème Anglaise onto individual dessert plates. Warm a serving spoon in hot water and then dip the spoon into the mousse to make an oval-shaped scoop. Put scoops, round side up, on the Crème Anglaise. To decorate, pipe lines of melted chocolate on top, using a toothpick to pull it into a pattern.

Baking dish
8in (20cm) gratin or other shallow dish

Makes
6 servings

Storage
Keeps for 1 week, covered, in the refrigerator

* **Warning**
This recipe contains uncooked egg whites (see page 9)

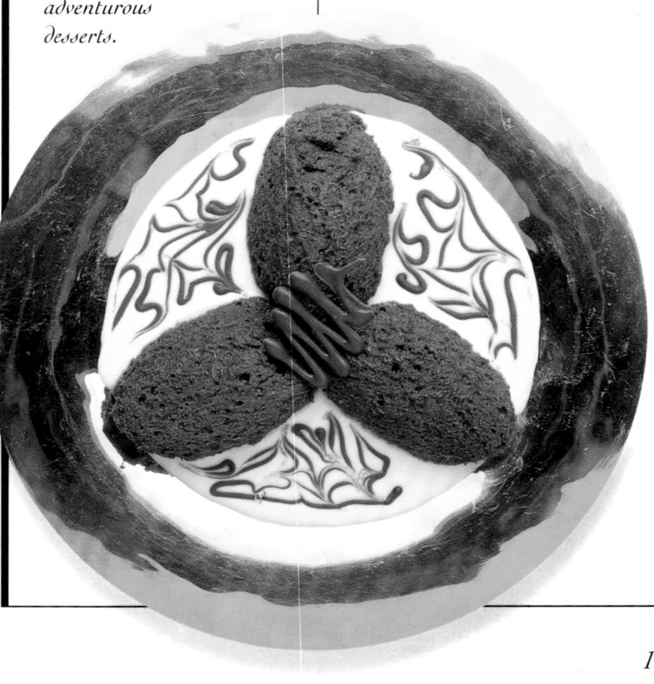

Marbled Millefeuilles
(See page 47.)

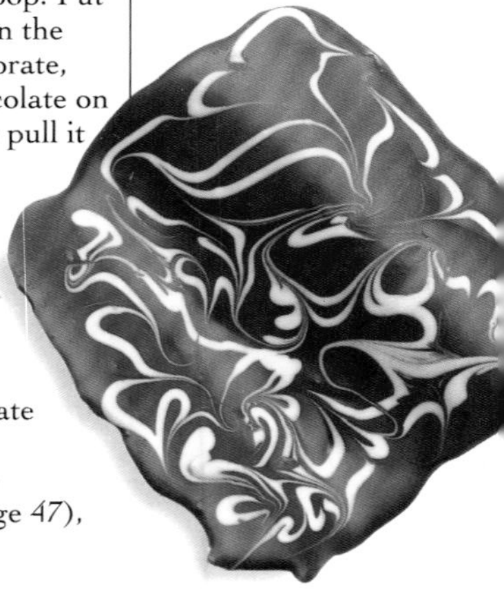

VARIATION
Marbled Millefeuilles
Put spoonfuls of Chocolate Velvet Mousse between marbled plain and white chocolate waves (see page 47), stacking them up as you would a layer cake.

MARBLED MILLEFEUILLE *sets creamy Chocolate Velvet Mousse between crisp waves of semisweet and white chocolate.*

Chocolate waves are shaped over wooden-spoon handles

Chocolate Velvet Mousse spooned between chocolate waves 3in (7cm) square

White Chocolate and Lime Mousse

In this deliciously simple mousse, the soft, creamy flavor of white chocolate contrasts with the marvelous tang of fresh limes – smoother and less tart than lemon.

INGREDIENTS

1½ tsp gelatin
2 tbsp cold water
8oz (250g) white chocolate, chopped (see page 32)
⅔ cup (150ml) heavy cream
5 tbsp (75ml) lime juice
rind of 1 lime, grated
2 egg whites
pinch of salt
2 tsp superfine sugar
lime zest, to decorate

1 Sprinkle the gelatin over the water in a cup and leave for 5 minutes to turn spongy. Put the cup in a bowl of hot water and let the gelatin dissolve.

2 Carefully melt the chocolate (see page 33). Whip the cream until it forms soft peaks. Stir a large spoonful of cream into the chocolate. Add the gelatin, lime juice, and rind and fold in the remaining cream.

3 Whisk the egg whites with the salt until they form soft peaks. Add the sugar and whisk for 30 seconds more. Fold a large spoonful of egg whites into the chocolate, then fold in the remaining whites.

4 Either leave the mixture in the bowl or spoon it into the ramekins and chill for 4–6 hours. To serve, leave the mousse in the ramekins or put spoonfuls from the large bowl into Chocolate Hazelnut Tuile baskets (see page 89). Decorate with twists of lime zest.

 Baking dishes
Six ramekins (optional)

 Makes
6 servings

Storage
Keeps for 2 days in the refrigerator

* **Warning**
This recipe contains uncooked egg whites (see page 9)

Chocolate Charlotte

The traditional charlotte is given a sophisticated touch here with the addition of chocolate and coffee.

INGREDIENTS

6oz (180g) bittersweet chocolate
10 tbsp (150g) unsalted butter, cut into small pieces
6 tbsp (45g) cocoa powder
2 eggs
⅓ cup (90g) superfine sugar
1–2 tbsp white rum
1¼ cups (300ml) heavy cream, whipped
small cup of strong black coffee
approx. 11oz (325g) ladyfingers

1 Melt the chocolate (see page 33). While still warm, whisk in the butter, then the cocoa.

2 Whisk the eggs and sugar over a bowl of hot water until the mixture is very thick and leaves a ribbon trail when the whisk is lifted. Using a metal spoon, carefully fold in the chocolate mixture, rum, and whipped cream.

3 Brush coffee on the flat side of the ladyfingers and line the bottom and sides of the mold, cutting the ladyfingers to shape where necessary, and placing the brushed side inward. Spoon the chocolate mixture into the mold, cover with plastic wrap, and chill in the refrigerator overnight.

4 An hour before serving, turn the charlotte out onto a dessert plate and leave at room temperature.

 Baking dish
6½in (17cm) diameter, 6¼ cup (1.5 liter) capacity, charlotte mold, lined with plastic wrap, leaving an overlap at the top

Makes
10 servings

Storage
Keeps for 3–4 days in the refrigerator

* **Warning**
This recipe contains lightly cooked eggs (see page 9)

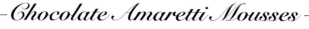

Chocolate Amaretti Mousses

These delectable individual mousses need only the simplest decoration, such as the crushed cookies I have suggested here.

INGREDIENTS

5oz (150g) semisweet chocolate

2 tbsp rum or brandy

2 tbsp strong black coffee

1 tbsp cocoa powder

4 eggs, separated

⅔ cup (150ml) heavy cream, whipped

1 cup (60g) crushed amaretti cookies

1 Melt the chocolate, rum, coffee, and cocoa powder together (see page 34). Stir until the mixture is smooth. While the mixture is still warm, whisk in the egg yolks, one at a time.

2 Whisk the egg whites, preferably in a copper bowl, until they are stiff. Fold a quarter of the whites into the chocolate to lighten the mixture, then fold in the remainder. Whip the cream until it holds soft peaks and fold into the chocolate mousse.

3 Put a heaping tablespoon of the crushed amaretti cookies on a piece of plastic wrap, seal, and set aside for decoration.

4 Put the remaining cookie crumbs evenly in the bottom of the ramekins and fill with the mousse. Chill in the refrigerator for 3–4 hours before serving, sprinkled with the reserved cookie crumbs.

Baking dishes
Eight ramekins

Makes
8 servings

Storage
Keeps for 2 days in the refrigerator

Freezing
2 months

* Warning
This recipe contains lightly cooked eggs (see page 9)

Iced Chocolate Soufflés

The plain exterior of these soufflés disguises a very rich dessert, for it contains two forms of chocolate, a generous splash of liqueur, and plenty of whipped cream.

INGREDIENTS

¼ cup (30g) cocoa powder

2oz (60g) semisweet chocolate, chopped (see page 32)

½ cup (125ml) water

⅓ cup (100g) superfine sugar

2 egg whites

2 tbsp Grand Marnier or white rum

1¼ cups (300ml) heavy cream, whipped

chocolate curls, to decorate (see page 42)

1 Melt the cocoa, chocolate, and 4 tablespoons of the water together (see page 34).

2 Dissolve the sugar and the remaining water in a small, heavy-based saucepan, bring to a boil, and boil without stirring until the temperature reaches the soft ball stage (240°F/115°C on a candy thermometer). While the sugar is boiling, whisk the egg whites until stiff.

3 Pour the hot sugar syrup in a steady stream over the whites, while continuing to whisk, and keep whisking until the mixture is thick and cool, about 10 minutes.

4 Fold the chocolate into the whites using a large metal spoon, and then fold in the alcohol and the whipped cream. Spoon into the ramekins and freeze for at least 3 hours, until the mousses are firm.

5 Before serving, remove the ramekins from the freezer and leave them in the refrigerator to soften for about 1½ hours. Peel away the paper collars and decorate the soufflés with chocolate curls.

Baking dishes
Four ramekins, each with a baking parchment collar extending 1½in (3.5cm) above the top of the ramekin

Makes
4 servings

Freezing
2 weeks, if completely wrapped

* Warning
This recipe contains lightly cooked egg whites (see page 9)

Chocolate Meringue Sandwiches

This excellent dinner party dessert is a clever combination of two recipes found in this book.

INGREDIENTS

For the meringues

1 quantity Chocolate Meringues (see page 81)

For the filling and decoration

1 quantity chocolate bavarois (see below)

⅔ cup (150m) heavy cream, whipped

½ cup (60–90g) raspberries

chocolate curls (see page 43)

1 Spoon the Chocolate Meringue mixture into a pastry bag fitted with a ¼in (5mm) plain tube.

2 Fasten the corners of the prepared baking parchment to the baking sheets with dabs of butter. Starting from the inside of the marked circles, pipe the mixture in coils.

3 Bake the meringues in the preheated oven for 1–1½ hours, or until crisp. Peel the meringues off the paper and put on a wire rack to cool.

4 Make the chocolate bavarois and pour it into the prepared pan. Chill until set.

5 Turn the bavarois out onto waxed paper. Peel away the baking parchment. Cut eight 3in (7cm) rounds from the bavarois. Sandwich the bavarois rounds with whipped cream between two meringues. Decorate with cream, raspberries, and chocolate curls.

Oven temperature
250°F/120°C

Baking time
1–1½ hours

Baking pans
Two flat baking sheets, lined with baking parchment, each marked with eight 3in (7cm) circles with ½in (1cm) spaces between; 11in (28cm) shallow baking pan, lined with baking parchment

Makes
8 meringues

Storage
Keep for 2 days in the refrigerator

Chocolate Bavarois Dessert

Chocolate-flavored bavarois – a light mousse set with gelatin – is given the glamour treatment here, set in a case made from chocolate-striped sponge cake.

INGREDIENTS

For the sponge case

1¼ cups (165g) all-purpose flour

2 tbsp cocoa powder

6 eggs, separated

½ tsp vanilla extract

¾ cup (190g) superfine sugar

¼ cup (30g) confectioners' sugar

2 tbsp orange marmalade, heated with 1 tbsp water

For the chocolate bavarois

¾ tbsp gelatin

4 tbsp fresh orange juice

¾ cup (175ml) milk

3 eggs, separated

⅓ cup (90g) superfine sugar

2 tbsp cocoa powder, sifted

2oz (60g) bittersweet chocolate, chopped into small pieces (see page 32)

pinch of salt

⅓ cup (90ml) heavy cream, lightly whipped

2 tbsp orange liqueur

For the decoration

white chocolate curls (see page 43)

strips of crystallized peel (see page 127)

1 For the sponge case, sift ½ cup (75g) of flour with the cocoa onto waxed paper. Sift the remaining ¾ cup (90g) of flour onto a second piece.

2 Whisk the egg yolks, vanilla, and all but 2 tablespoons of the sugar together until the mixture is thick and forms a ribbon when the whisk is lifted.

3 Whisk the whites until they form soft peaks, add the remaining sugar, and beat for another minute until firm.

4 Fold a spoonful of whites into the yolk mixture to loosen it, then carefully fold in the remaining whites. Before the whites are completely blended, scoop half of the mixture out into another bowl. Sift the flour and cocoa mixture over one bowl and fold in. Sift the flour over the other bowl and fold in.

5 Spoon the mixtures into two pastry bags fitted with ½in (1cm) plain nozzles. Pipe them

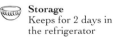

Oven temperature
425°F/220°C

Baking time
7–8 minutes

Baking pans
12 x 15in (30 x 38cm) flat baking sheet, greased, floured, and lined; 9 x 2½in (23 x 6cm) springform pan

Makes
8 servings

Storage
Keeps for 2 days in the refrigerator

* Warning
This recipe contains lightly cooked egg whites (see page 9)

alternately in diagonal lines on the baking sheet (see step 1, below). Dust with confectioners' sugar; dust again after 5 minutes.

6 Bake in the preheated oven for 7–8 minutes. Leave on the sheet for a few minutes, then turn out and peel off the paper (see step 2, below).

ASSEMBLING THE DESSERT

1 Measure and cut two strips of cake to line the side of the pan. Cut around to line the base (see step 3, below). Fit the pieces into the pan (see step 4, below). Brush with marmalade.

2 For the chocolate bavarois, put the gelatin and orange juice in a cup and leave for 5 minutes for the gelatin to turn spongy. Set the cup in hot water until the gelatin has dissolved.

3 Meanwhile, bring the milk to boiling point in a large saucepan. Beat the egg yolks

with 4 tablespoons of the sugar and the cocoa. Whisk the boiling milk into the egg mixture, then pour back into the saucepan. Cook over low heat, stirring, until the mixture begins to thicken and just coats the spoon. Do not allow it to come near a simmer, or it will curdle.

4 Remove from the heat and stir in the gelatin and chocolate. Whisk the egg whites and salt until they form soft peaks, add the remaining sugar, and whisk for 30 seconds, until the whites are stiff. Fold into the hot chocolate custard.

5 Put the bowl in ice water and turn the mixture occasionally while it thickens. When it starts to set, fold in the whipped cream and liqueur.

6 Pour the bavarois into the cake-lined pan and chill for at least 4 hours. Remove from the pan and decorate with chocolate curls and crystallized peel.

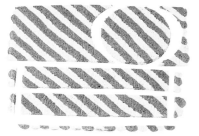

A striped sponge cake case for a rich dessert

How to make the sponge case

1 To make the striped sponge case, pipe alternate strips of plain and chocolate sponge diagonally across the baking sheet.

2 To peel the lining paper neatly off the sponge cake, lift up a corner farthest away from you and peel it back toward you.

3 For the lining, cut strips 2½in (6cm) wide for the side strips; cut the base slightly smaller than that of the 9in (23cm) cake pan.

4 To make the sponge case, fit the side pieces first, trimming to fit, then put in the bottom piece.

A slice of the elegant Chocolate Bavarois Dessert

Mont Blanc

Another delicious recipe using meringues, this one marries chestnuts and chocolate into a rich, creamy topping for the meringue base.

INGREDIENTS

For the meringues

2 egg whites
pinch of cream of tartar
½ cup (125g) superfine sugar
½ tsp vanilla extract

For the purée

1lb (500g) fresh chestnuts, cooked and peeled, or canned
1¼ cups (300ml) milk
2 tbsp superfine sugar
6oz (180g) semisweet chocolate, chopped
1 tsp vanilla extract
1¼ cups (300ml) heavy cream, whipped
2oz (60g) semisweet chocolate, grated (see page 42)

1 Make the meringue mixture (see page 81), pipe ten circles 3in (7cm) in diameter on the baking sheets, and bake in the preheated oven, all as for Chocolate Meringue Sandwiches (see page 110).

2 Simmer the chestnuts, milk, and the sugar together for 10 minutes. Pour into a food processor, add the chocolate and vanilla, and process until puréed; alternatively, use a food mill fitted with a large-hole disk.

3 Spoon the purée into a pastry bag fitted with an ⅛in (3mm) plain tube. (Add extra milk if the purée seems too thick to pipe.) Pipe purée around the edge of each meringue, to make a nest shape. Spoon whipped cream in the center. Sprinkle grated chocolate over the top. Chill until ready to serve.

VARIATION
Omit the meringue circles and work the purée through a food mill fitted with a large-hole disk directly onto a large serving plate. With the food mill close to the plate, let the strands fall around the outside edge of the dish. Raise the mill as you move toward the center of the dish, creating a cone-shaped mound. Cover with whipped cream, sprinkle with grated chocolate, and serve.

Oven temperature
250°F/120°C

Baking time
1–1½ hours

Baking pans
Two flat baking sheets, lined with baking parchment, each marked with five 3in (7cm) circles with ½in (1cm) spaces between

Makes
10 servings

Storage
Purée keeps for 2 days in the refrigerator; complete dessert keeps for 3–4 hours in the refrigerator

Petits Pots au Mocha et Chocolat

Serve these chocolate creams stylishly decorated for maximum effect: the rosette of whipped cream on this mocha petit pot is topped with a coffee bean.

INGREDIENTS

For the mocha petits pots

1¼ cups (300ml) light cream
2 tbsp medium-ground coffee
2oz (60g) semisweet chocolate, chopped (see page 32)
1 tbsp superfine sugar
4 egg yolks

For the chocolate petits pots

1¼ cups (300ml) heavy cream
6oz (180g) semisweet chocolate, chopped (see page 32)
1 tsp vanilla extract

1 For the mocha petits pots, bring the cream and ground coffee slowly to a boil, remove from the heat, stir a few times, and strain through a fine sieve or coffee filter paper.

Whisk in the chocolate and sugar until smooth. Whisk in the egg yolks, one at a time.

2 Divide the mixture among four ramekins and put in a roasting pan. Pour in hot water to come two-thirds up the sides of the ramekins. Cover the pan with foil. Bake in the preheated oven for about 30 minutes, or until just set. Cool, then chill for 30 minutes before serving.

3 For the chocolate petits pots, bring the cream to a boil, remove from the heat, and whisk in the chopped chocolate. When the mixture is smooth, stir in the vanilla. Divide the mixture among four ramekins, cool, and chill in the refrigerator for at least 3 hours.

Oven temperature
300°F/150°C

Baking time
30 minutes

Baking dishes
Eight ramekins

Makes
8 servings

Storage
Keep for 2 days, covered, in the refrigerator

Striped Silk

This elegant dessert requires no decoration other than a pretty serving plate. Serve a sweet cookie with it, such as Chocolate Hazelnut Tuiles (see page 89), if desired.

INGREDIENTS

3 envelopes (25g) gelatin
8 tbsp (120ml) cold water
4½ cups (1 liter) milk
8 egg yolks
½ cup (125g) superfine sugar
2oz (60g) semisweet chocolate, chopped (see page 32)
2 tsp vanilla extract
3 tbsp granulated sugar
1½ cups (350ml) heavy cream, whipped

1 Place the gelatin and 6 tablespoons (90ml) of the cold water in a cup and leave for 5 minutes for the gelatin to turn spongy. Set the cup in hot water until the gelatin has dissolved.

2 In a large saucepan, bring the milk to a boil. In a large bowl, whisk the egg yolks with the superfine sugar until the mixture is pale yellow. Gradually pour the hot milk over the egg yolks, whisking constantly, then return to the pan and stir with a wooden spoon over low heat until the custard thickens enough to coat the spoon lightly. Do not allow it to come near a simmer, or the eggs will curdle. Remove from the heat and stir in the gelatin.

3 Divide the custard among three bowls, preferably stainless steel. Stir the chocolate into one bowl. Add the vanilla extract to the second bowl.

4 Place the granulated sugar in a small heavy-based saucepan and heat until the sugar melts and caramelizes. Swirl the pan when the sugar colors and take it off the heat when it becomes a rich brown caramel. The caramel must be well browned, or it will be too sweet, but do not let it burn or it will turn bitter. Add the remaining 2 tablespoons of water to the caramel at arm's length to avoid splashes. Stir it over low heat to blend, then stir it into the third bowl.

5 When the custards have cooled, place the vanilla custard in ice water. When it starts to thicken, fold in one-third of the whipped cream.

ASSEMBLING THE MOLD

1 Rinse the mold in cold water and shake out the excess. Spoon in the vanilla cream and chill in the refrigerator or set in the freezer.

2 Set the caramel custard in ice water and, when it thickens, fold in half the remaining whipped cream. When the vanilla cream has set, but is not firm, spoon the caramel cream over the top and return the mold to the refrigerator or freezer.

3 Fold the remaining cream into the chocolate custard and spoon it on top of the firm caramel cream. Cover the mold and chill in the refrigerator for at least 4 hours.

SERVING THE STRIPED SILK

To serve the Striped Silk, dip the mold in very hot water for a few seconds. Slip a knife around the edge and invert it onto a serving plate, giving it a good shake if necessary to release the mold. Use a sharp knife when slicing and two spatulas to help slide the slices onto dessert plates.

NOTE: If your mold is a metal one and worn, it may impart a metal taste to the cream. Line it with plastic wrap or lightly oiled baking parchment.

 Baking dish
9 cup (2 liter) charlotte or other mold

 Makes
12 servings

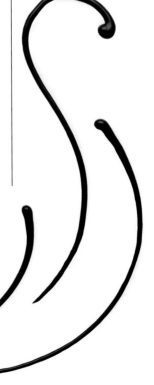 **Storage**
Keeps for 2 days, covered, in the refrigerator

Three-Chocolate Terrine

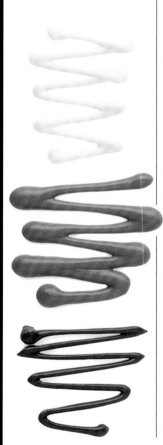

Three layers, three different textures: this terrine uses semisweet and white chocolate to create the maximum effect.

INGREDIENTS

For the cake layer

4 tbsp unsalted butter
3 tbsp cocoa powder
1 egg
½ cup (100g) superfine sugar
½ tsp vanilla extract
¼ cup (30g) all-purpose flour

For the white chocolate layer

1 tsp gelatin
6 tbsp (90ml) cold water
2 tbsp corn syrup
8oz (250g) white chocolate, chopped (see page 32)
2 egg yolks
pinch of salt
1¼ cups (300ml) heavy cream, lightly whipped

For the semisweet chocolate layer

1½ tsp gelatin
3 tbsp cold water
5oz (150g) semisweet chocolate
2 eggs, separated
2 tbsp rum
pinch of salt
⅓ cup (90ml) heavy cream, lightly whipped

1 For the cake layer, melt the butter over low heat, stir in the cocoa, and set aside. Whisk the egg with the superfine sugar, then stir in the cocoa mixture and the vanilla. Sift the flour over the top and fold in.

2 Pour the mixture into the prepared square cake pan and bake in the preheated oven for 20 minutes. Slide a knife around the inside edge of the pan and leave until cool before turning out onto a wire rack.

3 Cut a piece of cake to fit the bottom of the loaf pan and place in the bottom of the pan.

4 For the white chocolate layer, put the gelatin and 2 tablespoons of the cold water in a cup for 5 minutes for the gelatin to turn spongy. Put the cup in hot water and leave until the gelatin has dissolved.

5 Bring the remaining water with the corn syrup to a boil, remove from the heat, and stir in the white chocolate and gelatin. When the mixture is smooth, stir in the egg yolks and salt.

6 Lightly whip the cream and carefully fold into the mixture. Pour into the loaf pan and spread evenly. Chill for about 1 hour, or until nearly set.

7 For the semisweet chocolate layer, put the gelatin and the water in a cup and let turn spongy. Set the cup in hot water until the gelatin has dissolved.

8 Melt the semisweet chocolate (see page 33). While it is still hot, stir in the egg yolks and rum. Add the dissolved gelatin. Whisk the egg whites and salt until stiff. Fold into the chocolate. Lightly whip the cream and fold it into the mixture.

9 Spoon the dark chocolate mousse carefully over the white chocolate layer, spread it level, cover with plastic wrap, and return the loaf pan to the refrigerator for about 8 hours, until the terrine is set.

SERVING THE TERRINE

1 Lift the terrine out of the pan by the plastic wrap. Carefully peel away the plastic wrap, then cut the terrine into thin slices with a hot, dry knife.

2 Put the slices on dessert plates. If desired, serve with Bitter Chocolate Sauce (see page 135).

Oven temperature
350°F/180°C

Baking time
20 minutes

Baking pans
8in (20cm) square cake pan, buttered and floured; 10 x 4½in (25 x 11cm) loaf pan, lined with plastic wrap, leaving an overlap at the top

Makes
10–12 servings

Storage
Keeps for 2–3 days, covered, in the refrigerator

Freezing
2 months

Black and White Hazelnut Mousse

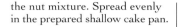

Crunchy hazelnut meringue gives extra texture to this layered dessert, which includes two chocolate mousses, dark and white.

INGREDIENTS

For the meringue

1 cup (125g) hazelnuts, toasted and skinned (see page 38)
1 tbsp flour
¼ cup (60g) superfine sugar
2 egg whites
pinch of cream of tartar

For the chocolate mousses

1½ tsp gelatin
6 tbsp (90ml) cold water
5oz (150g) white chocolate
2 egg yolks
pinch of salt
6oz (180g) bittersweet chocolate
6 tbsp (90g) unsalted butter, cut into small pieces
1 tsp vanilla extract
1¼ cups (300ml) heavy cream, lightly whipped

1 For the meringue, grind the nuts with the flour and half the sugar. Whisk the egg whites with the cream of tartar until firm, then whisk in the remaining sugar until they form stiff peaks. Fold in the nut mixture. Spread evenly in the prepared shallow cake pan.

2 Bake in the preheated oven for 20 minutes. Slip a knife around the edge, and leave for 5 minutes. Invert the meringue onto a wire rack, peel off the paper, and let cool.

3 For the mousses, put the gelatin with 4 tablespoons of the cold water in a cup and leave for 5 minutes for the gelatin to turn spongy. Put the cup in hot water and leave until the gelatin has dissolved.

4 Melt the white chocolate (see page 33). Stir 1 egg yolk, a pinch of salt, half the gelatin, and the remaining 2 tablespoons of water into the warm, melted white chocolate. Cool in the refrigerator.

5 Melt the semisweet chocolate (see page 33). Stir the butter, remaining gelatin and egg yolk, and vanilla into the warm, melted chocolate. Chill briefly.

6 Fold half the whipped cream into the white chocolate mixture and half into the semisweet chocolate mixture.

7 Cut the meringue into two lengths to fit the loaf pan. Put one layer in the pan and spread the dark chocolate cream over the top in an even layer. Put the second meringue on top and spread it with the white chocolate. Cover and chill for at least 5 hours.

8 An hour before serving, remove the mousse from the pan and cut into slices with a hot, dry knife. Put the slices on dessert plates and leave in a cool place. Serve with Raspberry Coulis (see page 137) and fresh raspberries.

 Oven temperature
350°F/180°C

Baking time
20 minutes

Baking pans
12 x 8in (30 x 20cm) shallow cake pan, lined with baking parchment; 10 x 3in (25 x 7cm) hinged loaf pan, lined with plastic wrap, leaving an overlap at the top

Makes
12 servings

Storage
Keeps for 3 days in the refrigerator

Freezing
The mousses freeze for 1–2 months

Step ahead
Make the meringue up to 1 week ahead; store in an airtight container

Marquise au Chocolat Blanc

This recipe combines a light sponge cake with a white chocolate mousse for a light-as-air summertime dessert. Use the egg whites not needed here to make meringues.

✳ Warning
This recipe contains uncooked egg yolks (see page 9).

INGREDIENTS

For the cake

¼ cup (90g) all-purpose flour
pinch of salt
3 eggs
⅓ cup (90g) superfine sugar
1 tsp vanilla extract
3 tbsp butter, melted

For the mousse

1 tsp gelatin
7 tbsp (100ml) cold water
2 tbsp corn syrup
10oz (300g) white chocolate, chopped (see page 32)
pinch of salt
3 egg yolks
1½ cups (350ml) heavy cream

1 For the cake, sift the flour and salt three times. Break the eggs into a large heatproof bowl and gradually beat in the sugar, using an electric hand-held beater. Set the bowl over hot water and beat for about 8 minutes, until the mixture has doubled in volume.

2 Sift the flour over the mixture, a third at a time, folding in each batch carefully with a large metal spoon. Fold in the vanilla and melted butter.

3 Turn the mixture into the prepared pan and bake in the preheated oven for 35 minutes. Run a knife around the inside of the pan to loosen the cake, leave for 5 minutes, then turn out onto a wire rack to cool.

4 For the mousse, put the gelatin and 2 tablespoons of the water in a cup for 5 minutes to turn spongy. Put the cup in very hot water and leave until the gelatin has dissolved.

5 Bring the remaining water and the corn syrup to a boil, remove from the heat, and stir in the chocolate, salt, and gelatin. When the mixture is smooth, stir in the egg yolks.

6 Lightly whip the cream and carefully fold into the mixture. Pour into the prepared loaf pan and cover with the cake, cut to fit. Chill overnight to set.

7 To serve, turn the marquise out and remove the plastic wrap. Cut it into slices with a hot, dry sharp knife. Bitter Chocolate Sauce (see page 135) makes an excellent accompanying sauce.

Oven temperature
350°F/180°C

Baking time
35 minutes

Baking pans
8in (20cm) square cake pan, buttered and floured; 8¾ x 4¼in (22 x 10½cm) loaf pan, lined with plastic wrap

Makes
10 servings

Chocolate Cones

These delightfully crisp cones should be filled before serving, in the same way as brandy snaps. Whipped cream, plus a few berry fruits, would be simple but delicious. A more extravagant filling is suggested at the end of the recipe.

INGREDIENTS

¼ cup (50ml) corn syrup
4 tbsp butter
¼ cup (60g) superfine sugar
⅓ cup (45g) all-purpose flour
2 tbsp cocoa
1 tbsp lemon juice

1 Melt the syrup, butter, and sugar together gently. Sift the flour and cocoa and stir into the mixture. Stir in the lemon juice.

2 Put 5 heaping tablespoons of the mixture onto each of

the prepared baking sheets, leaving room for spreading. Bake in batches in the preheated oven for 7–8 minutes per batch.

3 Cool on the baking sheets for 2 minutes. Working quickly, lift off and form into cones around metal or paper cones.

TO FILL THE CONES
For a rich filling, mix 1 cup (250g) mascarpone, flavored with 2 tablespoons sweetened strong coffee, and ⅔ cup (150ml) heavy cream.

Oven temperature
375°F/190°C

Baking time
7–8 minutes per batch

Baking pans
Two flat baking sheets, lined with baking parchment

Makes
10 cones

Storage
Keep for 2–3 days in an airtight container

Double Chocolate Festive Dessert

The Festive Dessert cuts easily into elegant slices

Tiny slices of chocolate swiss roll make a pretty tortoiseshell covering for this scrumptious dessert, filled with white chocolate mousse – a special creation for a special occasion.

INGREDIENTS

For the sponge cake

½ cup (60g) self-rising flour

¼ cup (30g) cocoa powder

3 eggs

⅓ cup (100g) superfine sugar

For the apricot filling

1 tsp gelatin

¾ cup (175ml) cold water

⅔ cup (180g) dried apricots

⅔ cup (150ml) heavy cream

For the white chocolate mousse

14oz (425g) white chocolate

½ cup (125ml) cold water

2½ cups (600ml) heavy cream

2–3 tbsp milk

1 For the sponge cake, sift the flour and cocoa three times. Set aside. Whisk the eggs and sugar in a bowl over a pan of hot water until the mixture is thick and leaves a ribbon trail when the whisk is lifted.

2 Sift the flour mixture over the eggs, a quarter at a time, folding in each addition with a large metal spoon. Pour the batter into the prepared pan and spread evenly.

3 Bake in the preheated oven for 12–15 minutes. Leave in the pan for 1 or 2 minutes, then turn out onto a piece of baking parchment lightly sprinkled with superfine sugar. Peel off the baking paper, lay it back over the cake, and replace the pan. Leave for at least 10 minutes.

4 For the apricot filling, put the gelatin and 2 tablespoons of the water in a cup and leave to turn spongy. Set the cup in hot water and leave until the gelatin dissolves.

5 Simmer the apricots with the remaining water, covered, until the apricots are soft and the water has

evaporated. Blend the apricots and gelatin to a purée in a food processor or blender, add the cream, and blend again.

ASSEMBLING THE DESSERT

1 Cut the cake into two layers (see page 50). Carefully lift off the top layer and place on a piece of baking parchment. Spread the apricot filling thinly over the cut sides of both layers. Roll each layer of cake tightly from the long side and wrap in the parchment. Freeze for several hours, or until very firm.

2 Cut the frozen cake into ¼in (5mm) slices, using a sharp knife, and line the prepared mold with them. Press the slices together so that there is no space between them. Set the lined mold and any unused slices aside.

3 For the white chocolate mousse, melt the chocolate and water together (see page 34). Let cool. Whip the cream to the soft peak stage. Fold the cream carefully into the cooled chocolate, a third at a time, adding the milk if the mixture looks grainy or is difficult to blend.

4 Spoon the mousse into the cake-lined mold. Cover with a layer of the remaining slices of cake and pull over the plastic wrap to cover tightly. Chill the dessert for at least 4 hours before serving.

Oven temperature
400°F/200°C

Baking time
12–15 minutes

Baking pans
12½ x 9½in (31 x 24cm) jelly roll pan, lined with baking parchment; 9 cup (2 liter) pudding bowl or mold, lined with plastic wrap, leaving an overlap at the top

Makes
14–18 servings

Storage
Keeps for 2 days in the refrigerator

Freezing
2 months

Ice Creams

Ices have been a passion in northern Italy for centuries. From there, Catherine de Medici's chefs introduced them to the French court in the 16th century. By the 17th century, the word had spread to England, brought by Italian chefs who were also opening cafés in Paris to sell ices and, later, ice creams. It was Italians, once again, who took ice cream to North America in the early 19th century. Today, ice cream is just as much a treat as ever, particularly when it is made at home with real cream, fresh eggs, and milk.

Chocolate Praline Ice Cream

An excellent chocolate ice cream to keep in the freezer, this has been given a crunchy texture by the addition of almond praline. If you prefer a smooth ice cream, omit the praline.

INGREDIENTS

3½oz (100g) praline (see page 51)

For the ice cream

6oz (180g) semisweet chocolate

2 cups (450ml) milk

5 egg yolks

½ cup (125g) superfine sugar

1¼ cups (300ml) heavy cream, lightly whipped

1 Make the whole praline recipe and store it ready for use. Melt the chocolate (see page 33) and set it aside to cool.

2 Bring the milk almost to a boil. Whisk the egg yolks with the sugar until thick and light, then whisk in the milk.

3 Return the mixture to the saucepan and continue to cook over low heat, stirring constantly with a wooden spoon, until the custard thickens enough to coat the spoon and leave a trail when your finger is drawn across the back of the spoon. Do not allow it to come near a simmer, or it will curdle.

4 Stir the chocolate into the custard and strain into a bowl. Chill until cool, then fold in the whipped cream. Freeze the mixture in an ice cream machine. Alternatively, put it in the freezer at the lowest setting until set around the sides and bottom. Take it out and beat vigorously, then return to the freezer. Repeat the process. Before the ice cream has set, stir in 3½oz (100g) of the praline and return to the freezer.

SERVING THE ICE CREAM
Serve the ice cream in chocolate baskets (see page 44), and decorated with piped shapes (see page 47). Add flecks of edible gold foil.

 Makes
4½ cups (1 liter); 6–8 servings

Freezing
2–3 months

Melted chocolate pipes easily into decorative shapes

For a sparkling effect, add tiny pieces of edible gold foil

CHOCOLATE PRALINE ICE CREAM

This is a luxurious ice cream, based on an egg custard. Very satisfying served simply, it also lends itself to being turned into an extravagantly presented showstopper.

Elegantly piped chocolate patterns decorate the ice cream

Chocolate-Coated Ice Cream Balls

This is a great excuse for using the ice creams already stored in the freezer.

INGREDIENTS

*1 quantity
Chocolate Praline Ice Cream
(see page 118)
or White Chocolate Ice Cream
(see below),
or a mixture of both*

8oz (250g) semisweet chocolate

1 Put the prepared baking sheet in the freezer for 10 minutes. Take small round balls from the ice cream with an ice cream scoop and put them on the cold baking sheet. You should have 24–30 balls.

2 Put the tray back in the freezer for about 2–3 hours, until the balls are very hard.

3 Melt half the chocolate (see page 33). Leave until lukewarm. Roll half the balls, one at a time, in the chocolate and put back on the baking sheet. Return to the freezer as soon as possible.

4 Repeat with the remaining chocolate and ice cream balls, remelting the chocolate if it starts to harden. Serve the balls the day you make them.

 Equipment
Flat baking sheet, lined with baking parchment

 Makes
8 servings

White Chocolate Ice Cream

This is a beautifully creamy ice cream. Give it dinner party glamour by serving it in chocolate baskets (see page 44), with piped chocolate fans (see page 46).

INGREDIENTS

12oz (375g) white chocolate

3½ cups (800ml) milk

¾ cup (180g) granulated sugar

5 eggs

1 Melt the chocolate with 6 tablespoons (90ml) of the milk (see page 34) and set aside. Pour the rest of the milk into a heavy-based saucepan, add half the sugar, and slowly bring the mixture to a boil.

2 Meanwhile, beat the eggs and remaining sugar until the mixture is pale and thick. When the milk comes to a boil, pour it over the eggs in a slow steady stream,

beating constantly. Return to the saucepan and stir slowly with a wooden spoon, over medium heat, until the custard thickens just enough to coat the spoon and leave a trail when your finger is drawn across the back of the spoon. Do not let the custard come near a simmer, or it will curdle.

3 Remove from the heat and whisk in the chocolate. Let the mixture cool in an ice water bath.

4 Freeze the cold mixture in an ice cream machine, or use the freezer method (see page 118). Store in the freezer in a covered container until needed.

Makes
8–10 servings

Freezing
2–3 months

Chocolate Sorbet

An ice rather than an ice cream, this chocolate sorbet is good served with a sweet cookie, such as Chocolate Hazelnut Tuiles (see page 89).

INGREDIENTS

2 cups (500ml) water

½ cup (125g) granulated sugar

½ cup (60g) cocoa powder

2oz (60g) bittersweet chocolate, chopped (see page 32)

1 Put all the ingredients in a saucepan and bring to a boil, stirring occasionally. Take off the heat and let cool.

2 Freeze the mixture in an ice cream machine until set. Alternatively, use the freezer method (see page 118).

3 Take the mixture from the freezer, chop into several pieces, and process in the chilled bowl of a food processor or blender until well blended. Return to the freezer for at least another 2 hours before serving.

 Makes
6–8 servings

Freezing
2–3 months

Chocolate Semifreddo

A generous dash of a coffee-flavored liqueur, such as Tia Maria, Kahlúa, or crème de café, adds a touch of the exotic to this light chocolate ice.

INGREDIENTS

1½ cups (350ml) heavy cream

¾ cup (125g) confectioners' sugar

4 egg whites

3oz (90g) bittersweet chocolate, grated

5 tbsp coffee-flavored liqueur

1 Whip the cream with half the sugar until it forms soft peaks. Whisk the egg whites until stiff, then whisk in the remaining sugar for a few seconds more until they are thick and glossy.

2 Fold the whites into the cream, then fold in the chocolate and liqueur. Spoon the mixture into the prepared pan and spread evenly. Cover and freeze for at least 8 hours.

3 To serve, lift the Semifreddo out of the pan, using the overlap of plastic wrap. Peel off the plastic wrap, cut the Semifreddo into slices, and serve on individual plates.

Equipment
10 x 4½in (25 x 11cm) loaf pan, lined with plastic wrap, leaving a good overlap at the top

Makes
8 servings

Freezing
2 months

Warning
This recipe contains uncooked egg whites (see page 9).

Passion Fruit Surprise Bombe

An ice cream bombe always looks impressive, and this one, made with a delicious passion fruit ice cream, packs an extra surprise.

INGREDIENTS

juice of 1 lemon

½ cup (125ml) orange juice

1 tsp gelatin

2 egg whites

¼ tsp cream of tartar

¾ cup (180g) superfine sugar

8 passion fruit

1¼ cups (300ml) heavy cream

7oz (200g) semisweet chocolate

1 Strain the lemon juice into a measuring cup. Add enough orange juice to make ½ cup (125ml) of juice. Sprinkle the gelatin over the juice and leave until spongy.

2 Whisk the egg whites with the cream of tartar until they form stiff peaks.

3 Scrape the gelatin mixture into a saucepan, add the sugar, and heat gently until dissolved. Increase the heat and boil rapidly for 3 minutes. Pour in a thin stream onto the egg whites, whisking constantly at high speed. Continue whisking for several minutes, until cool and thickened.

4 Cut the passion fruit in half, scoop out the insides, and put in a blender. Blend for 45 seconds to detach the membranes from the seeds. Strain through a sieve into a bowl, working as much of the juice and pulp through the sieve as possible.

5 Whisk the cream until it is thick but not stiff. Whisk in the passion fruit juice and pulp. Using a large metal spoon, gently fold the cream into the egg white mixture.

6 Transfer to the mold or basin. Spread the mixture up the sides, leaving a slight dip in the center. Freeze for at least 5 hours, until firm.

7 When the ice cream is firm, coarsely grate the chocolate (see page 42). Scoop out the center of the ice cream and set aside. Fill the cavity with the chocolate. Stir the reserved ice cream to soften it and spread over the chocolate. Return to the freezer for at least 1 hour.

8 Dip the mold briefly in very hot water, loosen the edges with a narrow spatula, and turn the bombe out onto a serving plate. Return to the freezer until you are ready to serve it.

Equipment
5 cup (1.2 liter) metal bombe mold

Makes
8 servings

Freezing
2 months

Chocolate Truffles

Truffles are sinfully easy to make and warrant the best chocolate you can find. They can be flavored with your favorite liqueur, and you could add candied orange zest or diced marrons glacés to some of the truffles, instead of the praline suggested in the recipe. Special chocolate bars, such as those flavored with tea and spices, can also be used for making more unusual truffles.

INGREDIENTS

1 cup (200ml) light cream
2 tbsp butter
8oz (250g) bittersweet chocolate, broken into pieces
8oz (250g) semisweet chocolate, broken into pieces
2 tbsp rum, Cognac, or liqueur of your choice (optional)
1oz (30g) praline (see page 51)
For the coating
4 tbsp cocoa powder, sifted with 1 tbsp confectioners' sugar
chocolate vermicelli
praline (see page 51)

1 Heat the cream and the butter in a heavy-based saucepan until it reaches a rolling boil. Remove the mixture from the heat and stir in both chocolates, stirring until the mixture is smooth.

2 Add the liqueur, if using, then pour the mixture into the prepared pan and spread out with a narrow spatula. Leave in a cool place, uncovered, for 24 hours to firm up.

3 To make the truffles, pull marble-size pieces from the mixture in the pan and roll them in the palms of your hands to shape into balls. Add praline to some of the truffles, if desired.

COATING THE TRUFFLES
1 Prepare the chosen coatings. Sift the cocoa and confectioners' sugar onto baking parchment or waxed paper; sprinkle the other coatings onto flat plates.

2 Roll a few truffles in each coating, using different coatings for different flavors.

PIPING THE TRUFFLES
An alternative way of completing the truffles is to pipe the mixture into foil candy cups, painted on the inside with a coating of melted chocolate. Put the mixture, while still creamy, into a nylon pastry bag fitted with a small star nozzle and pipe it into the cases. Leave to firm up. Peel away the cases.

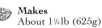

Equipment
Shallow cake pan or jelly roll pan, lined with baking parchment

Makes
About 1¼lb (625g)

Storage
Keep for 2 weeks in the refrigerator, layered between baking parchment in a covered container

How to coat truffles in chocolate

1 *Take marble-size pieces of the truffle mixture and roll lightly into balls between the palms of the hands. Make sure your hands are cool and dry.*

2 *To coat a truffle in chocolate, turn it in the melted chocolate with a fork. Lift it from the bowl, scraping the fork against the rim so that excess chocolate falls back into the bowl.*

3 *Put the coated truffles on a piece of baking parchment or waxed paper, spaced well apart, to allow the chocolate to set.*

White Chocolate Truffles

White chocolate truffles have a uniquely rich taste. To keep their creamy color, try coating them in white couverture or rolling them in finely grated white chocolate, as an alternative to the cocoa suggested here.

INGREDIENTS

6oz (180g) white chocolate, broken into pieces

5 tbsp (75g) unsalted butter, diced

3 tbsp heavy cream

pinch of salt

½ tsp orange liqueur

2 tbsp sifted cocoa powder, to coat

1 Melt the chocolate, butter, cream, and salt together (see page 34). Remove from the heat and let cool. When the mixture has cooled, add the orange liqueur. Cover and chill in the refrigerator until firm, about 2 hours.

2 Pull marble-size pieces off the chilled mixture and roll them in the palms of your hands to shape into balls. If the mixture becomes difficult to handle, return to the refrigerator and chill further.

3 Put the cocoa on a piece of waxed paper; roll the truffles in it to coat them evenly.

 Makes
About 30 truffles

 Storage
Keep for 2 weeks in the refrigerator, layered between baking parchment in a covered container

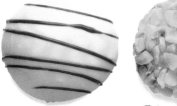

Chocolate-Covered Nuts

Chocolate and nuts are a wonderful combination. Pecans, almonds, and walnuts are particulaly good if they are caramelized before being coated with chocolate. I tell you how to do this at the end of this recipe.

INGREDIENTS

1½lbs (750g) couverture chocolate or 1½ lbs (750g) semisweet chocolate and 1 tbsp sunflower or peanut oil

3 cups (375g) toasted and skinned hazelnuts (see page 38) or macadamia nuts

1 Temper the couverture (see page 35). Alternatively, melt the semisweet chocolate and oil together (see page 34). For best results, the couverture chocolate should be 88–90°F (31–32°C) before being used for coating.

2 Make a large paper piping bag (see page 46). Fill it with some of the melted chocolate. Snip a hole in the cone and squeeze out 40 half-teaspoon-size drops onto one of the prepared baking sheets.

3 Arrange three nuts in a triangle on top of each chocolate drop and let set.

4 Remelt the remaining chocolate, if necessary. Using a fork, submerge a nut cluster in the chocolate. Lift out and scrape gently on the edge of the bowl to shake any excess chocolate back into the bowl.

5 Put the nut clusters on the second prepared baking sheet to dry. Repeat with the remaining nuts.

NOTE
To caramelize nuts, heat 1 cup (250g) sugar in a heavy-based saucepan, stirring constantly, until pale caramel in color. Take the pan off the heat and use a fork to dip the nuts, one at a time, in the hot syrup. Lay them on a lightly oiled baking sheet to set.

    If the caramel becomes too thick, reheat it over very low heat. The caramelized nuts must be cold before being used in the recipe.

 Equipment
Two flat baking sheets, lined with baking parchment

Makes
About 40 candies

Storage
Keep for 2 weeks, stored in an airtight container

Panforte di Siena

INGREDIENTS

1 cup (125g) candied orange and lemon peel, chopped

2 tbsp brandy

1 cup (125g) unblanched almonds

1 cup (125g) unblanched hazelnuts

1 cup (125g) all-purpose flour

2 tbsp cocoa powder

2 tsp ground cinnamon

½ tsp ground coriander

½ tsp ground allspice

½ cup (150g) granulated sugar

⅔ cup (150ml) dark liquid honey

1 tbsp confectioners' sugar mixed with ½ tsp cinnamon

*P*anforte – the Italian word translates as "hard bread" – is really a sweet, and a very special one, packed full of nuts, honey, candied peel, and spices. In Siena the windows of many shops are stacked high with beautifully wrapped disks of Panforte. It keeps well and makes an attractive gift, particularly when wrapped in Florentine-style paper.

1 Mix the peel and brandy in a mixing bowl and set aside.

2 Bring a small saucepan of water to a boil. Add the almonds and bring back to a boil. Lift an almond out with a slotted spoon and squeeze it to see if it will peel easily. If it does, drain and peel the almonds. If it doesn't, boil for another minute. Peel the almonds.

3 Place the almonds in one shallow pan and the hazelnuts in another and bake in an oven preheated to the higher temperature for about 8 minutes. Shake the pans occasionally so the nuts toast evenly. Remove the nuts from the oven; reduce the oven temperature to the lower setting. Rub the hazelnuts in a cloth to remove the skins.

4 Chop the hazelnuts and the almonds very roughly and mix into the peel. Sift the flour, cocoa, and spices together and stir into the peel.

5 Put the sugar and honey in a small, heavy-based saucepan. Stir over low heat until the syrup comes to a boil, then boil without stirring until the syrup reaches 260°F (127°C), measured on a candy thermometer.

6 Pour the hot syrup over the nut and peel mixture and stir to blend. Pour into the prepared pan and bake for 40 minutes. Remove from the oven and set on a wire rack to cool.

7 When partially cool, sprinkle with the confectioners' sugar and cinnamon. Remove the Panforte from the pan when cold and leave in a dry place for several days to firm up. It should be chewy but firm enough to stay flat and be cut into slices.

Oven temperature
350°F/180°C;
then
275°F/140°C

Baking time
40 minutes

Baking pan
8in (20cm) round shallow cake pan, greased and lined with baking parchment

Makes
One 8in (20cm) round

Storage
Keeps for 4 months, wrapped in foil, in an airtight container

Rocky Road

*C*hildren enjoy this North American candy made with milk chocolate, nuts, and marshmallows. The bumpy surface explains the name.

INGREDIENTS

12 marshmallows

¾ cup (90g) walnuts or pecans

1lb (500g) milk chocolate, chopped (see page 32)

1 Dice the marshmallows and roughly chop the nuts. Melt the chocolate (see page 33).

2 Stir the marshmallows and nuts into the chocolate and pour onto the prepared baking sheet. With a lightly oiled narrow spatula, smooth over the surface, covering any nuts and marshmallows with the chocolate.

3 Let the mixture set for 1–1½ hours in the refrigerator before breaking it into small pieces.

VARIATION
Substitute 1 cup (125g) dried banana chips for the marshmallows and nuts and follow the recipe.

Equipment
Flat baking sheet, lined with baking parchment

Makes
About 1¼lb (625g)

Storage
Keeps for 2 weeks in the refrigerator

Chocolate Buttercrunch

INGREDIENTS

2 cups (250g) unblanched almonds

1 cup (250g) granulated sugar

4 tbsp water

1 cup (250g) unsalted butter,
cut into small pieces

1 tbsp lemon juice

8oz (250g) semisweet chocolate

When I was a teenager living in New York City, there was a chain of confectionery shops called Loft's that made a delicious buttercrunch candy. Years later, I was delighted to find I could make this very similar version.

1 Finely chop one-third of the nuts and set aside. Roughly chop the remaining two-thirds.

2 Place the sugar and water in a heavy-based saucepan and stir over low heat until the sugar has almost dissolved. Add the butter and continue to stir until the mixture has blended.

3 Add the roughly chopped nuts and cook over moderate heat, stirring occasionally, until the mixture reaches 300°F (150°C), measured on a candy thermometer.

4 The syrup should turn a caramel color, but it must be watched with great care at this stage to prevent it from sticking and burning.

5 The moment the mixture reaches the correct temperature, remove it from the heat, stir in the lemon juice, and quickly pour it into the prepared pan.

6 Before the buttercrunch sets, lift it out of the pan and score the top into 1½in (4cm) squares with a sharp knife. When it is cold, carefully peel away the lining paper and cut or break the buttercrunch into neat squares.

7 Melt the chocolate (see page 33). Spread the reserved finely chopped nuts on a square of waxed paper. Spread the tops of the squares with chocolate, then press into the nuts. Cover the bottoms of the buttercrunch in the same way.

8 Allow the chocolate to set before storing the buttercrunch, between layers of baking parchment or waxed paper, in an airtight container.

 Equipment
8in (20cm) square cake pan, bottom and sides lined with baking parchment

Makes
About 1¼lb (625g)

Storage
Keeps for 2 weeks in an airtight container

Chocolate Pomelo Candies

INGREDIENTS

2 pomelos or grapefruit or
3 large oranges

4½ cups (1 liter) water

1lb (500g) granulated or superfine sugar

6oz (180g) semisweet chocolate

The pomelo (also called shaddock) is a very large citrus fruit. Its peel is particularly good for candying. Its flavor is intense and, once candied, it has an attractive translucent appearance.

1 Wash and dry the fruit. Use a small sharp knife to make four slits from the top to bottom at quarterly intervals. Remove the peel in leaf-shaped sections. Put the peel in a saucepan, cover with plenty of boiling water, and simmer for 10 minutes. Refresh in cold water, then repeat the boiling and refreshing process as many times as necessary to reduce the citrus bitterness to a level you find palatable.

2 Dissolve the sugar in the water over low heat, add the peel, and simmer gently for 1½ hours, until the peel is soft. Remove the peel from the syrup and put on a wire rack to dry. Drain in a strainer, then on paper towels until cool.

3 Melt the chocolate (see page 33). Cut the peel into thin batons. Spear each piece of peel with a wooden toothpick and dip it in the chocolate, either halfway or to coat the whole piece. Stick the toothpick into a potato until the chocolate sets.

 Makes
1lb (500g)

Storage
Keep for 3 weeks in an airtight container

Peppermint Creams

A favorite after-dinner treat. Oil of peppermint, which can be bought at pharmacies, gives a result far superior to that of peppermint flavoring.

INGREDIENTS

1½ cups (375g) granulated sugar

½ cup (125ml) water

1 tsp lemon juice

6–8 drops oil of peppermint

5–6oz (150–180g) semisweet chocolate, to coat

1 Put the sugar, water, and lemon juice in a heavy-based saucepan. Stir carefully over moderate heat to dissolve the sugar. Brush down the sides of the pan with a pastry brush dipped in water to dissolve any grains of sugar.

2 Boil until the syrup reaches 240°F (115°C), measured on a candy thermometer. Remove from the heat and add the peppermint oil.

3 Pour onto a damp work surface. Allow to cool for several minutes before working with a damp spatula in a figure-eight motion. Work the mixture for about 10 minutes, until it is opaque and stiffens slightly. If it is still quite soft, leave for 30 minutes to become firmer.

4 Drop teaspoons of the fondant onto baking parchment. Set aside until cold.

5 Coat the fondants in semisweet chocolate, as for Armagnac Prune Truffles (see page 122).

Makes
About 1lb (500g)

Storage
Keep for 2 weeks in an airtight container

Chocolate Mint Crisps

These can be whipped up in minutes and are perfect to serve with after-dinner coffee.

INGREDIENTS

4oz (125g) semisweet chocolate

6 drops oil of peppermint

1 tbsp light brown sugar

1 Melt the chocolate (see page 33). Leave until it is slightly cool to the touch but still liquid. Add the oil of peppermint and the sugar. Taste, adding more oil of peppermint if you want the crisps to have a stronger, more minty flavor.

2 Pour the mixture onto the prepared baking sheet and spread out to make a rectangle measuring about 6½ x 9in (16 x 23 cm). Before it sets, score the chocolate into 1½in (3.5cm) squares. When it is firm and cool, cut it into squares.

Equipment
Two flat baking sheets, lined with baking parchment

Makes
About 24 candies

Storage
Keep for 2 weeks in an airtight container

Chocolate Fudge

Fudge is always a great favorite with children – and with adults.

INGREDIENTS

1¾ cups (425g) granulated sugar

1 cup (250ml) milk

1 tbsp corn syrup

6 tbsp (90g) unsalted butter

2oz (60g) semisweet chocolate

6 tbsp (45g) cocoa powder

1 tsp vanilla extract

½ cup (60g) walnuts, chopped

1 Put the sugar, milk, and corn syrup into a heavy-based saucepan and stir together over moderate heat until the sugar dissolves. Cook without stirring until the temperature reaches 238°F (114°C), measured on a candy thermometer.

2 Meanwhile, melt the butter, chocolate, and cocoa together (see page 34). When the syrup has reached the correct temperature, pour in the chocolate mixture. Stir in the vanilla and nuts and pour into the prepared pan.

3 Cut the fudge into small squares when it has set.

Equipment
8in (20cm) square shallow cake pan, lined with baking parchment

Makes
About 1¼lb (625g)

Storage
Keeps for 2 weeks in an airtight container

Chocolate Eggs

You can present these chocolate-filled eggshells innocently masquerading as fresh hens' eggs. To make an assortment of chocolate eggs, use plastic egg molds, available in various sizes. The molds can be filled with alternate spoonfuls of white and semisweet chocolate to give a marbled effect. Once unmolded, the egg halves can be stuck together with a little melted chocolate.

INGREDIENTS

6 small eggs
10oz (300g) bittersweet chocolate
¾ cup (175ml) heavy cream
3oz (90g) praline, finely ground (see page 51)
2 tbsp white rum (optional)

1 With a needle, pierce a small hole in the pointed end of each egg. Use small scissors to enlarge the hole to a circle about ½in (1cm) in diameter. Shake the raw egg out into a bowl and reserve for another use. Pour running water into the shells and shake until they are clean and empty. Dry the shells in a low oven for 10 minutes.

2 Melt the chocolate (see page 33). Bring the cream to a boil in a small saucepan, remove from the heat, and stir in the chocolate. Stir in the praline and rum. Spoon or pipe the mixture into the eggshells until full. Wipe any chocolate off the outer shells and chill until firm. Seal the holes with a small round label and place in an egg carton or small basket with the labels at the bottom.

VARIATION

Crack the shells of the filled eggs and peel off. Decorate the chocolate eggs with narrow ribbons, or wrap them in colored foil.

Makes
6 eggs

Storage
Keep for 2 weeks in the refrigerator

Marbled Chocolate Eggs, made in plastic molds, sit in a nest of chocolate curls

Savory Chocolate

Chocolate was first used in South America as a drink spiced with chilies. Even after the Spanish sweetened its naturally bitter flavor, chocolate continued to be used in Europe, particularly in Italy and Spain, to enhance certain savory dishes. The recipes here, which come from Europe and Mexico, show the great versatility of chocolate as a savory ingredient, combining it with poultry, game, and seafood, as well as the Aztecs' chilies.

Mole de Guajolote

The word "mole", from the Mexican Indian word molli, *means a sauce made from chilies. I have chosen a moderately hot version, but you can easily raise or lower the heat by adjusting the amount of chilies.*

Enhance the flavor of the chilies by heating them before soaking overnight. Heat in a heavy-based pan for 3 minutes to soften them.

INGREDIENTS

6 mulato chilies, seeded
6 ancho chilies, seeded
4 pasilla chilies, seeded
8lb (4kg) turkey, cut into portions
1 onion, quartered
5 garlic cloves, crushed
1½ tsp salt
½ cup (60g) sesame seeds
1 cup (125g) blanched almonds
2 corn or flour tortillas
3 mild onions, chopped
5 tomatoes, peeled and chopped
⅓ cup (60g) raisins
6 black peppercorns
2 cloves
½ tsp aniseed
1 tsp ground cinnamon
4–6 tbsp sunflower oil
2–3oz (60–90g) semisweet chocolate
salt and freshly ground black pepper

1 Soak the chilies overnight in 4 cups (900ml) water.

2 Put the turkey pieces in a large saucepan with the onion and 2 garlic cloves, cover with water, and bring to a boil. Add the salt, cover, and simmer for 1 hour or until the turkey is just tender.

3 Cool, then take the turkey pieces out of the casserole, skin them, and cut the meat off the bones into neat pieces. Put the meat in a large flame-proof casserole. Return the skin and bones to the saucepan and simmer for another hour to concentrate the stock's flavor.

4 Set aside a few sesame seeds for garnish and toast the rest with the almonds in a dry skillet, tossing them over moderate heat until browned. Remove, then cook the tortillas in the hot pan for about 5 minutes, turning them, until they are hard and brittle. Break them into small pieces.

5 Put the soaked chilies and their water, the mild onions, remaining garlic, tomatoes, and tortillas in a processor or blender and work to a smooth paste. Transfer to a bowl.

6 Rinse out and dry the processor or blender and add the sesame seeds, almonds, raisins, peppercorns, and spices. Grind the mixture fine, then add it to the chili paste.

7 Heat the oil in a large sauté pan and fry the paste, stirring constantly, for about 5 minutes. Add to the casserole.

8 Measure out 2½ cups (600ml) of the stock and put it in a pan with the chocolate, broken into pieces. Heat until the chocolate has dissolved; pour into the casserole. Season to taste with salt and pepper. Simmer gently over very low heat, adding more stock if necessary, until the sauce is the consistency of heavy cream.

 Makes
12 servings

Storage
Keeps for 7 days in the refrigerator

Freezing
2–3 months

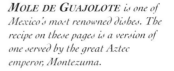

MOLE DE GUAJOLOTE *is one of Mexico's most renowned dishes. The recipe on these pages is a version of one served by the great Aztec emperor, Montezuma.*

SERVING THE MOLE DE GUAJOLOTE
Garnish the dish with the reserved sesame seeds or a green herb and serve it with white rice, cooked beans, and warm soft tortillas. Extra garnishes such as avocados, limes, and chilies add an exotic, colorful touch.

Vivid green flat-leaf parsley garnishes this Mexican dish

Venison Stew

A wonderful winter dish and special enough to be party fare. It improves with reheating, so can be made well in advance. It also makes an excellent filling for pies.

INGREDIENTS

2½lb (1.25kg) venison meat from the shoulder, off the bone

For the marinade

2 tbsp olive oil

1 carrot, chopped

1 large onion, sliced

1 celery stalk, chopped

1½ cups (375ml) red wine

For the stew

2 tbsp olive oil

4 shallots, finely chopped

4 garlic cloves, crushed and chopped

1¼ cups (300ml) beef stock

1 tbsp tomato paste

bouquet garni, made of 1 bay leaf, sprig of thyme, several stalks of parsley

10 juniper berries

10 peppercorns

strip of orange peel

1½ tbsp red currant jelly

1½oz (45g) bittersweet chocolate, grated (see page 42)

salt and freshly ground black pepper

1 Cut the meat into small cubes and put in a bowl.

2 For the marinade, heat the oil in a large skillet and gently cook the carrot, onion, and celery until lightly browned. Pour in the wine and remove from the heat. When the marinade is cool, pour it over the meat. Leave overnight in a cool place or in the refrigerator.

3 Next day, remove the venison from the marinade and pat it dry with paper towels. Reserve the marinade.

4 For the stew, heat the oil in a nonstick pan and brown the meat, in batches, on all sides. Remove the meat to a heatproof casserole. Add the shallots and garlic to the pan and stir over low heat until softened. Add them to the casserole.

5 Pour the marinade, with its vegetables, into the pan and stir, scraping up any brown bits from the bottom of the pan. Tip the marinade into the casserole and add the stock, tomato paste, bouquet garni, juniper berries, peppercorns, and orange peel.

6 Season lightly with salt, bring to a simmer on top of the stove, cover, and put in the preheated oven. Adjust the heat, if necessary, so the stew cooks very slowly – a bare simmer – for 2–2½ hours, until the meat is tender.

7 Strain the juices into a saucepan. Boil briskly to reduce by one-quarter. Whisk in the red currant jelly and the chocolate. Add pepper (and extra salt, to taste). Pour the sauce back over the stew and remove the bouquet garni. Serve it hot. A rutabaga or parsnip purée, chestnuts, and a green vegetable go well with this stew.

 Oven temperature
325°F/160°C

Cooking time
2–2½ hours

Makes
6 servings

Storage
Keeps for 2–3 days, covered, in the refrigerator

Calamares con Chocolate

The original Catalan dish on which this recipe is based uses baby octopus (pulpitos), but the more readily available squid is a good substitute.

INGREDIENTS

1½lb (750g) squid
3 tbsp olive oil
2 garlic cloves
⅓ cup (25g) slivered almonds
1 large mild onion, finely chopped
1 bay leaf
½ tsp dried thyme
1 cup (250ml) white wine
4 tomatoes, peeled and chopped
salt and freshly ground black pepper
pinch of saffron
½oz (15g) bittersweet chocolate, grated (see page 42)
2 tbsp finely chopped parsley

1 To prepare each squid, hold the sac firmly and pull off the head and tentacles. Cut the tentacles off and reserve. Extract the long bone from the sac and any gelatinous matter and discard. Rinse the sac under cold running water. Cut the sac into rings and the tentacles into pieces.

2 Heat 2 tablespoons of the oil in a sauté pan or skillet and cook the garlic and almonds until lightly browned. Transfer them to a mortar. Add the remaining oil to the pan and soften the onion in it, then add the squid, bay leaf, and thyme. When the squid turns opaque, pour in the wine. Reduce the sauce slightly, then add the tomatoes and salt and pepper. Cover and simmer gently until the squid is tender, about 1 hour.

3 Pound the almonds and garlic with the saffron to make a paste, thinning it with a little of the pan juices. Stir the paste into the squid, add the chocolate, and let the mixture heat through to thicken. Stir in the parsley. Serve with boiled new potatoes, to soak up the fragrant sauce.

Makes
4 servings

Storage
Keeps for 2–3 days, covered, in the refrigerator

Freezing
2–3 months

Conejo con Chocolate

Semisweet chocolate is used frequently to flavor game sauces in Spain. The amount of chocolate is relatively small, but it imparts a subtle, although difficult to identify, taste.

INGREDIENTS

4 tbsp olive oil
2 garlic cloves
1 rabbit, cut up
seasoned flour for coating
1 onion, sliced
1 carrot, sliced
sprig of thyme
1 bay leaf
small piece of cinnamon stick
1¼ cups (300ml) red wine
1 small glass dry sherry
salt and freshly ground black pepper
½ cup (45g) blanched almonds
3 tbsp pine nuts
1oz (30g) bittersweet chocolate, chopped (see page 32)
2 tbsp brandy
pinch of sugar (optional)

1 Heat the oil in a casserole and cook the garlic until lightly colored. Transfer with a slotted spoon to a mortar and set aside.

2 Toss the rabbit in the flour and cook until browned. Add the onion, carrot, thyme, bay leaf, and cinnamon. Stir briefly to distribute the vegetables, then pour in the wine and sherry. Season with salt and pepper. Bring to a boil and simmer gently, covered, for 40 minutes.

3 Pound the garlic with the almonds, pine nuts, chocolate, and a few tablespoons of pan juices, if necessary, to make a paste. Dilute with the brandy. Add to the rabbit and simmer a few minutes more. Taste for seasoning, adding a pinch of sugar if the sauce is too bitter. Serve with rice or potatoes.

Makes
4 servings

Storage
Keeps for 2–3 days, covered, in the refrigerator

Freezing
2–3 months

Sauces & Fillings

Add a richly flavored chocolate filling to a cake or a smooth sauce to a dessert, and you immediately lift them out of the everyday into the luxury class. The chocolate sauces and fillings here are perfect with chocolate-based recipes, but would also add an extra dimension to recipes that do not contain chocolate. As with any chocolate recipe, the success of a chocolate sauce or filling depends on the quality of the chocolate used. Always choose a chocolate with a high cocoa solid content and not too much sugar.

Chocolate Sauce

Here is an easy alternative to the Bitter Chocolate Sauce opposite. This one is made with cocoa powder.

INGREDIENTS
½ cup (60g) cocoa powder
1 cup (250ml) water
½ cup (125g) superfine sugar
2 tbsp butter

Simmer the cocoa, water, and sugar together, stirring, for 3 minutes. Stir in the butter and return to a simmer. Add more water, if necessary, to make a pouring consistency.

Makes
1¼ cups (300ml)

Storage
Keeps 2–3 days, covered, in the refrigerator

Crème Anglaise

Crème Anglaise, a light soothing custard, is very good served with a variety of chocolate desserts. It is also the base for many ice creams. It has to be made with care to ensure that the egg yolks, which thicken the milk, do not curdle.

INGREDIENTS
1¼ cups (300ml) milk
½ vanilla bean, split lengthwise, or 1 tsp vanilla extract
3 egg yolks
2 tbsp superfine sugar

1 Bring the milk almost to the boil, with the vanilla bean, if you are using it.

2 Beat the egg yolks with the sugar until thick and light, then whisk in the hot milk. Return the mixture to the pan and cook over low heat, stirring constantly with a wooden spoon, until the cream thickens slightly. Do not allow the mixture to come near a simmer, or it will curdle.

3 Strain into a bowl and let cool, when it will thicken more. Add the vanilla extract, if using, and refrigerate.

VARIATIONS:
Coffee Crème Anglaise: Add 1 tablespoon instant coffee, diluted in a little water, to the basic Crème Anglaise.
Mocha Crème Anglaise: Add 2oz (60g) grated semisweet chocolate and 1 teaspoon instant coffee to the thickened cream.
Liqueur Crème Anglaise: Add 1 tablespoon or more to taste of Poire Williams or Grand Marnier.

Makes
1½ cups (350ml)

Storage
Keeps 2–3 days in the refrigerator

Hot Fudge Sauce

This has a fine fudgy flavor, and is as good poured over ice creams as it is with hot puddings.

INGREDIENTS
½ cup (125ml) heavy cream
2 tbsp unsalted butter
5 tbsp (45g) cocoa powder, sifted
¼ cup (60g) superfine sugar
¼ cup (60g) dark brown sugar
pinch of salt

Place all the ingredients in a heavy-based saucepan. Stir over low heat until the mixture is smooth and melted. Increase the heat slightly and continue to cook the sauce for 2–3 minutes. If a sweeter sauce is desired, add more superfine sugar.

Makes
⅔ cup (150ml)

Storage
Keeps 1–2 days, covered, in the refrigerator

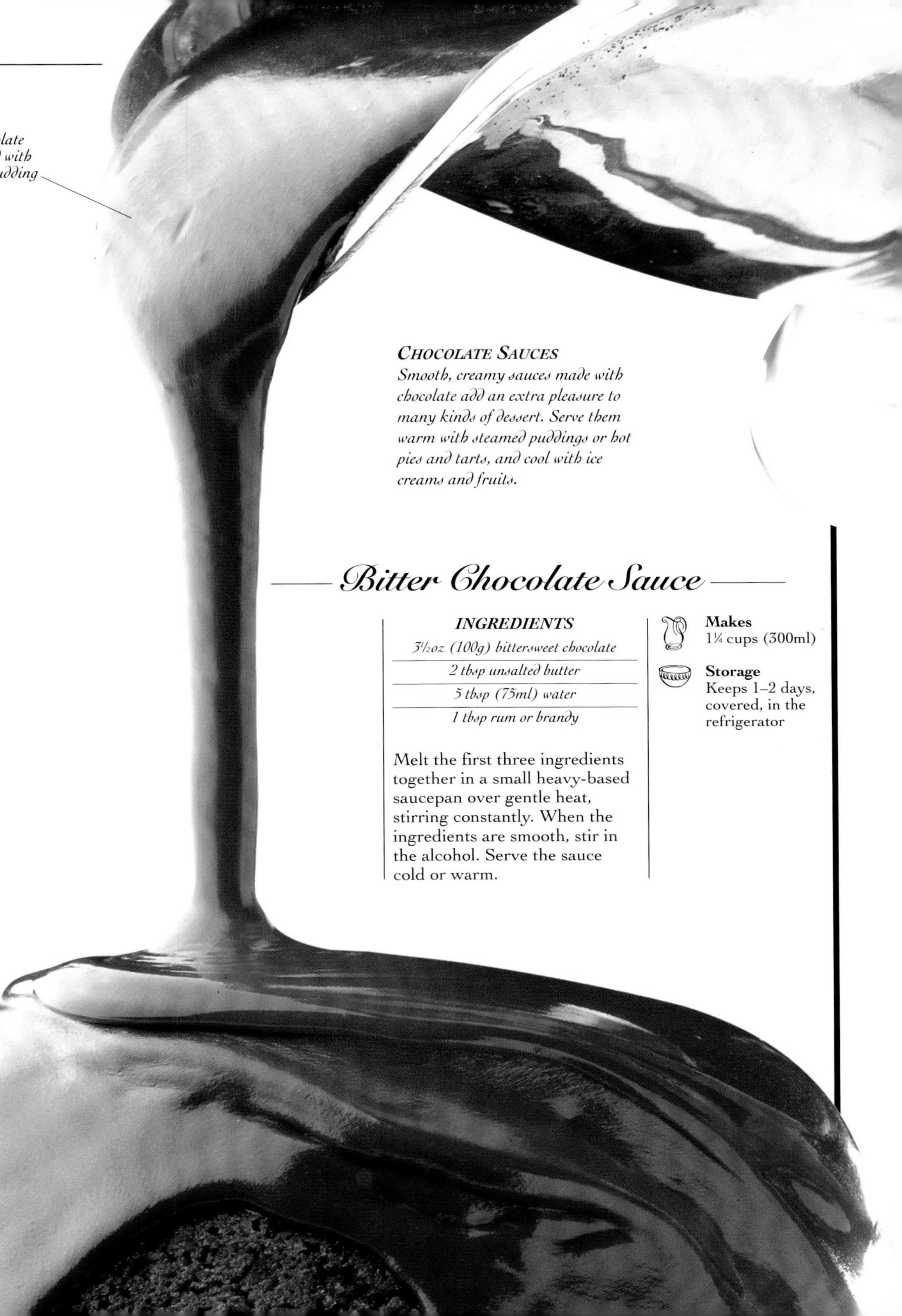

Bitter Chocolate
Sauce served with
a steamed pudding

CHOCOLATE SAUCES
Smooth, creamy sauces made with
chocolate add an extra pleasure to
many kinds of dessert. Serve them
warm with steamed puddings or hot
pies and tarts, and cool with ice
creams and fruits.

Bitter Chocolate Sauce

INGREDIENTS

3½oz (100g) bittersweet chocolate

2 tbsp unsalted butter

5 tbsp (75ml) water

1 tbsp rum or brandy

Melt the first three ingredients
together in a small heavy-based
saucepan over gentle heat,
stirring constantly. When the
ingredients are smooth, stir in
the alcohol. Serve the sauce
cold or warm.

Makes
1¼ cups (300ml)

Storage
Keeps 1–2 days,
covered, in the
refrigerator

Chocolate Ganache

This versatile chocolate cream can be used as a filling, an icing, and a sauce.

INGREDIENTS

5oz (150g) bittersweet chocolate, chopped (see page 32)

5oz (150g) semisweet chocolate, chopped (see page 32)

1¼ cups (300ml) heavy cream

1 Put the chocolate in a large bowl. Bring the cream to a boil, pour over the chocolate, and leave for 5 minutes. Whisk gently until the cream and chocolate are blended.

2 Continue to whisk until the ganache is fluffy and cool. Do not overbeat, or it will be too stiff to spread. If the ganache is to be used as a sauce, whisk only until it is blended and still warm.

Makes
Enough to fill and ice a 9in (23cm) two-layer cake; serves 8 as a sauce

Storage
Keeps for 2–3 days in the refrigerator

Chocolate Buttercream

Buttercream makes an excellent filling and icing for layer cakes. Its basic ingredients, as used in the Wedding Cake (see pages 66–7), are egg yolks, butter, water, and sugar. Here, I give a recipe for a plain chocolate buttercream. For a white chocolate buttercream, see the recipe for White Chocolate Cake (page 61).

INGREDIENTS

4 egg yolks

½ cup (125g) granulated sugar

½ cup (100ml) water

1 cup (250g) unsalted butter, chopped

3½oz (100g) bittersweet chocolate, melted (see page 33)

1 Beat the egg yolks in a bowl until they are pale and thick.

2 Gently heat the sugar and water in a heavy-based saucepan until dissolved. Bring to a boil and boil until the syrup reaches the soft ball stage, 240°F (115°C), measured on a candy thermometer.

3 Gradually pour the syrup over the egg yolks, beating with a hand-held electric mixer (avoid pouring the syrup over the beater's blades) until the mixture is thickened and tepid.

4 Beat the softened butter gradually into the mixture. Mix in the melted chocolate.

Makes
Enough to fill and ice a 9in (23cm) two-layer cake

Storage
Best used as soon as made

Chocolate Glaze

This is a rich, glossy icing for cakes. A simpler icing, based on cocoa, is given with the recipe for Eclairs (see page 83).

INGREDIENTS

3oz (90g) bittersweet chocolate

3oz (90g) semisweet chocolate

½ cup (125g) unsalted butter

1 tbsp corn syrup

1 Break both of the chocolates into small pieces.

2 Melt the chocolate pieces with the other ingredients in a heavy-based saucepan (see page 34).

3 Set the cake to be glazed on a wire rack over a large plate and pour the glaze over (see page 49).

Makes
Enough to glaze an 8–9in (20–23cm) cake

Apricot Filling

This creamy, fruity filling is excellent with chocolate cakes and roulades. Dried apricots have a high sugar content, so no extra sugar is needed here.

INGREDIENTS

1 tsp gelatin

¾ cup (175ml) water

¾ cup (180g) dried apricots

⅔ cup (150ml) heavy cream

1 Put the gelatin and 2 tablespoons of the water in a cup and let turn spongy. Put the cup in a bowl of hot water until the gelatin has dissolved.

2 Place the apricots with the remaining water in a heavy-based saucepan. Cover the pan, then simmer until the apricots are soft and the water has evaporated.

3 Blend the apricots and gelatin to a purée in a food processor, then add the cream to the mixture, and blend again for a smooth filling.

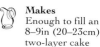

Makes
Enough to fill an 8–9in (20–23cm) two-layer cake

Raspberry Coulis

This sharp and fruity red sauce is delicious with all kinds of chocolate confections. It should be kept on the tart side to balance the sweetness of the dessert.

INGREDIENTS

1½ cups (300g) raspberries, fresh or frozen

⅓ cup (90g) superfine sugar

1 Put the raspberries and sugar in a bowl. Leave for at least 1 hour to allow the flavors time to develop.

2 Blend the fruit and sugar to a purée in a food processor (or beat with a whisk).

3 Rub the mixture through a fine sieve into a bowl, and press as much of the juice through as possible. Serve the coulis cold.

Makes
1¼ cups (300ml)

Storage
Keeps for 2 days in the refrigerator

Freezing
2 months

Orange Sauce

A quick sauce can be made from fresh blood orange juice. It has a strong, tart flavor that goes well with cakes or puddings rich in chocolate.

INGREDIENTS

2 tsp cornstarch

2 tbsp water

1¼ cups (300ml) freshly squeezed blood orange juice

sugar to taste (optional)

1 Put the cornstarch and water in a bowl and mix to a smooth paste.

2 Pour the orange juice into a small, heavy-based saucepan. Stir in the cornstarch paste.

3 Bring the mixture to a simmer, stirring constantly. Add sugar to taste, if needed. The sauce is best used as soon as it is made.

Makes
1¼ cups (300ml)

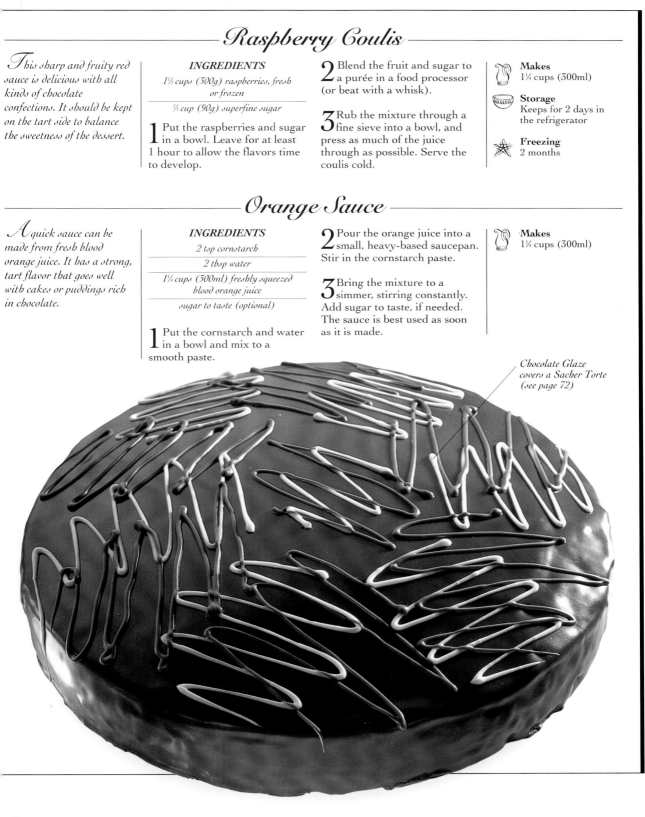

Chocolate Glaze covers a Sacher Torte (see page 72)

Chocolate Drinks

" 'Monsieur,' Madame d'Arestel, Superior of the Convent of the Visitation at Belley, once said to me more than fifty years ago, 'whenever you want to make a really good cup of chocolate, make it the day before, in a porcelain coffee pot, and let it set. The night's rest will concentrate it and give it a velvety quality, which will make it better. Our good God cannot possibly take offense at this little refinement, since he himself is everything that is most perfect'." – J. A. Brillat-Savarin, *Physiologie du goût* (1825).

Viennese Hot Chocolate

This delicious drink conjures up thoughts of the great days of the Austro-Hungarian Empire, when Vienna was the liveliest city in Europe.

INGREDIENTS
⅔ cup (150ml) heavy cream

3¾ cups (900ml) milk

3 tbsp superfine sugar

1 tbsp dark rum or Cognac

8oz (250g) bittersweet chocolate, finely chopped (see page 32)

1 Lightly whip the cream and set aside.

2 Heat the milk in a large saucepan until almost boiling. Remove from the heat and whisk in the sugar, rum, or Cognac, and all but 1 tablespoon of the chocolate.

3 Ladle into four cups and top with a dollop of whipped cream and a sprinkling of the remaining chocolate.

VARIATION
Mexican Hot Chocolate
For this version, omit the cream and stir in a pinch of ground cloves and ½ teaspoon ground cinnamon.

Makes
4 servings

Chocolate Float

When drugstores had soda fountains, this was one of their most popular drinks. Perhaps too much for today's taste, but as an occasional treat or pick-me-up it is hard to beat.

INGREDIENTS
1¼ cups (300ml) milk

2 heaping tbsp malted milk powder

2 heaping tbsp sweetened cocoa powder

4 heaping tbsp chocolate or vanilla ice cream

2 scoops chocolate ice cream

Whizz together in a blender the milk, malted milk powder, cocoa, and 4 tablespoons of ice cream. Divide the mixture between two tall glasses and serve with a scoop of chocolate ice cream floating in each one.

Makes
2 servings

Iced Chocolate

Use this recipe to make Café Liègeois: add a scoop of vanilla or chocolate ice cream to the Iced Chocolate and top with whipped cream and a sprinkling of cinnamon or cocoa.

INGREDIENTS
1 cup (250g) granulated sugar

1¼ cups (300ml) water

½ cup (60g) cocoa powder

2 tsp instant espresso coffee powder

5 cups (1.25 liters) milk

1 Dissolve the sugar in the water over low heat, then bring to a boil, and boil briskly for 3 minutes. Whisk in the cocoa and coffee powders.

2 Let cool, then chill in the refrigerator until ready to serve.

3 Pour ¼–⅓ cup (50–90ml) of the syrup into a glass and top off with milk. Serve in chilled glasses with ice cubes.

Makes
4–6 servings

COFFEE WITH CHOCOLATE

The affinity that chocolate has with coffee is well known. Chocolates served with after-dinner coffee are irresistible. A sprinkling of chocolate or cocoa over the milky froth of a cappuccino adds richness. A pinch of cocoa added to ground coffee, in whatever coffeemaker you use, will enhance its flavor. And for a special after-dinner treat, add a small square of chocolate to a heated cup, top with hot fresh coffee, add 1 teaspoon of brandy, and float a thin layer of cream over the top of the cup. Serve without stirring.

A small fan of chocolate, set in the whipped cream, is a final touch of luxury

VIENNESE HOT CHOCOLATE *is a wonderfully warming mixture of rich chocolate, cream, and milk, with a wicked dash of liqueur.*

The scoop of ice cream on top gives the Chocolate Float its name

CHOCOLATE FLOAT, *once a soda fountain special, is a splendidly cool way to drink chocolate.*

Montezuma

This is a fine drink for sipping after dinner on a summer evening, perhaps outside.

INGREDIENTS

2½ cups (600ml) milk

1 tbsp granulated sugar

3oz (90g) bittersweet chocolate

⅛ tsp cinnamon

⅛ tsp allspice

5 tbsp (75ml) rum

⅓ cup (90ml) brandy or Calvados

rind of ½ lemon, grated

cracked ice

1 Gently heat the milk, sugar, chocolate, cinnamon, and allspice together, and stir constantly until blended. Remove from the heat and let cool.

2 Transfer the milk mixture into a cocktail shaker, add the other ingredients, and shake. Pour into 4 glasses and serve very cold.

Makes
4 cocktails

Brandy Alexander

Crème de cacao, a popular chocolate-flavored liqueur, is used for many exotic cocktails. Those that include cream are best served after a meal or at a Christmas gathering in place of eggnog.

INGREDIENTS

ice cubes

½ cup (125ml) brandy

½ cup (125ml) crème de cacao

½ cup (125ml) heavy cream

freshly grated nutmeg

Put the ice cubes, brandy, crème de cacao, and heavy cream in a cocktail shaker. Shake well, then strain into four cocktail glasses. Grate nutmeg over the top of each and serve immediately.

VARIATIONS

Nureyev
Equal quantities of vodka and colorless crème de cacao.

Pavlova
Equal quantities of vodka, crème de cacao, and cream.

Pushkin
Equal quantities of vodka, gin, and crème de cacao.

Crow
Equal quantities of whisky or bourbon and crème de cacao, and a dash of orange bitters.

Makes
4 cocktails

Nureyev has a Russian touch

Crow includes whisky and crème de cacao

Addresses

Baking Ingredients
Broadway Panhandler
477 Broome Street
New York, NY 10013
Tel: (212) 966-3434
Speciality baking ingredients, including pastel chocolates. Mail and phone orders.

Durey-Libby Edible Nuts
100 Industrial Road
P.O. Box 345
Carlstadt, NJ 07072
Tel: (201) 939-2775
Fax: (201) 939 0386
Gourmet nuts: walnuts, pecans, cashews, almonds, pistachios, and macadamias sold in bulk for baking purposes. Mail and phone orders.

Festive Foods of the Rockies
P.O. Box 49172
Colorado Springs, CO 80949-9172
Tel: (719) 594-6768
Fax: (719) 522-1672
Belgian chocolate and other baking ingredients. Mail and phone orders.

Ghirardelli
1111 139th Avenue
San Leandro, CA 94578
Tel: (800) 877-9338
Full line of gourmet chocolate products. Call for catalog.

Guittard
P.O. Box 4308
Burlingame CA 94011-4308
Tel: (800) 468-2462
Manufacturer of quality bittersweet, semisweet, white, and milk

chocolates, chocolate coatings, and cocoa powder

Sweet Celebrations
P.O. Box 39426
Edina, MN 55439-0426
Tel: (800) 328-6722
Fax: (612) 943-1688
A range of imported and domestic chocolates, catalog and mail order.

Baking Equipment
Bridge Kitchenware
214 East 52nd Street
New York, NY 10022
Tel: (800)-BRIDGE K
Tel: (212) 838-1901, if calling from the New York area
Complete line of high-quality cookware, including cake pans and chocolate molds.

New York Cake and Baking Distributor
56 West 22nd Street
New York, NY 10010
Everything for baking: cake pans, chocolate molds, chocolates, gourmet baking ingredients, and more. Call for catalog.

Williams-Sonoma
P.O. Box 7456
San Francisco, CA 94120
Tel: (800) 541-2233
Tel: (415) 421-7900, if calling from the San Francisco area
Complete line of cookware. Call for catalog.

Acknowledgments

Author's Appreciation
I would like to thank the many people at Dorling Kindersley who have been responsible for producing this book, particularly Editorial Director Daphne Razazan, Managing Editor Fay Franklin, and the talented art editor Jane Bull. I give my special thanks to my editor, Janice Anderson, for the careful and excellent work she has done on the text. Thanks to photographer Ian O'Leary and his assistant Emma Brogi for the mouthwatering photographs. Janice Murfitt produced and styled all the recipes for the photographs, and I am greatly indebted to her for her fine and beautiful work. Many thanks to Zoë Keen and Bryony Miller, who helped me work on and test the recipes, Josceline Dimbleby for allowing me to use her Passion Fruit Bombe, and my good friend Nancy Lassalle for her help and the generous use of her kitchen in Cape Cod. Thanks also to my family for all their tasting and useful comments and to John Lowenthal for his measured advice and constant support.

Dorling Kindersley would like to thank Virginia Walter for design management, Paul Wood and Suzy Dittmar for DTP design, Julia Pemberton Hellums for editorial work, and Susan Bosanko for the index. Props were supplied by Tables Laid, China & Co., and Surfaces.

Picture Credits
Key to pictures: t = top, c = center, b = bottom, l = left, r = right.
The publisher would like to thank the following for their kind permission to reproduce the following photographs: Jean-Loup Charmet, Paris 6; Musée de Versailles/E. T. Archive 7; RBG Kew 8; Mary Evans Picture Library 9.
Photography by Ian O'Leary, except
Dave King 39, 42 br, 43 br, 45 br, 46 r, c, br, 48 ct, b, rt, rb, 51 c, bl, br, 82–3 bl, c, br; David Murray 32r.